The Power of the Written Tradition

SMITHSONIAN SERIES IN ETHNOGRAPHIC INQUIRY
William L. Merrill and Ivan Karp, Series Editors

Ethnography as fieldwork, analysis, and literary form is the distinguishing feature of modern anthropology. Guided by the assumption that anthropological theory and ethnography are inextricably linked, this series is devoted to exploring the ethnographic enterprise.

ADVISORY BOARD

Richard Bauman (Indiana University), Gerald Berreman (University of California, Berkeley), James Boon (Princeton University), Stephen Gudeman (University of Minnesota), Shirley Lindenbaum (City University of New York), George Marcus (Rice University), David Parkin (Oxford University), Renato Rosaldo (Stanford University), and Norman Whitten (University of Illinois)

Jack Goody

The Power of the Written Tradition

Smithsonian Institution Press
Washington and London

Copy editor: Susan A. Warga
Production editor: Ruth G. Thomson
Designer: Janice Wheeler

Library of Congress Cataloging-in-Publication Data
Goody, Jack.
    The power of the written tradition / Jack Goody.
        p.   cm.
    Includes bibliographical references (p.   ) and index.
    ISBN 1-56098-987-4 (cloth : alk. paper).—ISBN 1-56098-962-9 (paper :
alk. paper)
        1. Written communication.   2. Oral tradition.   3. Language and
culture.   4. Literacy.   5. Language and logic.   I. Title.
    P211.G664   2000
    302.2'244—dc21   99-41206

British Library Cataloguing-in-Publication Data are available

Manufactured in the United States of America
06 05 04 03 02 01 00   5 4 3 2 1

♾ The paper used in this publication meets the minimum requirements of the
American National Standard for Information Science—Permanence of Paper
for Printed Library Materials ANSI Z39.48-1984.

Contents

Acknowledgments   vii

1. Objections and Refutations   1

2. Memory in Oral Tradition   26

3. The Construction of a Ritual Text:
   The Shift from Oral to Written Channels   47

4. The Time of Telling and the Telling
   of Time in Written and Oral Cultures   63

5. Writing and Revolt in Bahia   86

6. Derrida among the Archives
   of the Written and the Oral   109

7. Canonization in Oral and Literate Traditions   119

8. Technologies of the Intellect:
   Writing and the Written Word   132

9. Power and the Book   152

Notes   167

References   171

Index   183

Acknowledgments

I have many personal debts to acknowledge in this field, principally to Ian Watt, Moses Finley, Michael Cole, and David Olson, but also to many others who have offered advice, criticism, or comments over the years. I would also like to thank Ruth Daniel for her help with the proofs.

Some of the studies that follow are published here for the first time; others have previously appeared elsewhere. Chapter 2 combines the article "Oral Cultures," published in *International Encyclopedia of Communications*, ed. E. Barnouw (New York: Oxford University Press, 1989, 226–29), with a piece given as a Darwin Lecture and published in *Memory*, ed. Patricia Fara and Karalyn Patterson (Cambridge: Cambridge University Press, 1998); chapter 4 was presented at a conference at the Stanford Humanities Center and is reprinted, with permission of the publishers, from *Chronotypes: The Construction of Time*, ed. J. Bender and D. Wellbery (Stanford: Stanford University Press, ©1991 by the Board of Trustees of the Leland Stanford Junior University); chapter 5 was published in *Visible Language* 20, no. 3 (1986): 318–43, and was given as the McLuhan Lecture, 1986, sponsored by Teleglobe Canada; chapter 6 arose from a contribution to a debate at the Centre Pompidou, Paris, in February 1995; chapter 7 was prepared for a conference at Leiden and is to be published in a volume edited by K. van der Toorn; chapter 8 arose out of a lecture given to the Smithsonian Institution, Washington, D.C.; and chapter 9 is based on a talk given at the Bibliothèque nationale de France, Paris. I thank the editors of the journals and books for permission to reprint, and thank the institutions that have supported my research and teaching in recent years, especially St. John's College, Cambridge; the Smithsonian Institution; the Whitney Humanities Center of Yale University; the Wissenschaftskolleg zu Berlin; and the British Council.

1
Objections and Refutations

Since 1968 I have published a number of books trying to relate my own experience and research, and those of others, in societies with and without writing. The present volume represents a continuation of that work over the last five years and is in part new and in part an expansion, clarification, and development of older themes. I am interested in two aspects of the power of the written word. The first is the power it gives to cultures that possess writing over purely oral ones, a power that enables the former to dominate the latter in many ways, the most important of which is the development and accumulation of knowledge about the world. That process involves changing certain aspects of our cognitive operations—the ways we understand and manipulate the world—in this case through the text, by means of what I call "technologies of the intellect." That obviously touches upon topics referred to under the rubrics of logic and rationality; I have discussed this elsewhere, most recently in the first chapter of my 1995 book *The East in the West*. I have tried to clarify a line of argument concerning these topics, as they give rise to a good deal of misunderstanding.

The other major theme relates to the power writing may endow upon various elements in a particular society. This involves not only the hegemonic power that the control of these means of communication provides to dominant groups, often religious ones; the dominated, too, may make use of this way of grappling with their social environment. A paradigmatic example of this is the limited use made of writing by the black slaves and freedmen of the Brazilian town of Bahia in the early nineteenth century. Other examples include the contributions made by women writers, from Sappho onward, to the cultural traditions of complex societies, whether these be the female poets of early Tamil Nadu, the women troubadours of the twelfth century, the author of *The Tale of Genji* in Heian Japan, or the women novelists in eighteenth- and nineteenth-century Europe and America.

It has been suggested that I need to make a synthetic reply to criticism of the "literacy hypothesis." There are four reasons I have been unwilling to do this. The first is that I prefer to get on with tackling new problems, or new aspects of old problems, rather than going over the same ground. The second is that such discussions tend to become personalized in terms of critics rather than criticism, whereas one should perhaps concentrate on the points of agreement, being flattered that others have thought the ideas worth a detour. The third is that I see the problem not as one of testing a general hypothesis, but as one of defining the implications of literacy and seeing how these relate to, and provide a better explanation of, the general theories, statements, assumptions, and categories of others. The fourth is that the subject is complex, many-stranded, the subject of much research in various fields, and best subject to synthetic review rather than contestatory debate at a generalized level.

In this volume I present a series of thoughts about the nature of the differences between cultures with writing and those without. The line of argument and the presentation of evidence develop a theme that I and others have previously proposed, stressing the transforming effects of literate activity on human life. That does not mean to say that we do not recognize the existence of embryonic forms of the syllogism, for example, in oral cultures, or of notions of proof and evidence; we imply only that these are eventually transformed in various ways by the advent of writing (as earlier of speech). Nor are all aspects of communication equally affected; orality remains a dominant form of human interaction, although itself modified in various ways by the addition of new means and modes of communication.

This line of argument has not been accepted by all scholars. Postmodernists, especially philosophers such as Jacques Derrida, downplay the notion of difference between the written and the oral by adopting metaphorical extensions of the terms of debate; cultural relativists such as the anthropologist Brian Street do the same from an antievolutionist, antihistorical perspective (Street 1985). The essays address some of these counterarguments. In this introduction I want to look at some of the propositions arising out of the cultural relativist stance, which has also been roundly criticized by other scholars, including the philosopher-anthropologist Ernst Gellner.

It is worth drawing more than passing attention to Derrida's discussion of "reading" the stars (see chapter 6). Clearly all societies interpret visual signs, such as footprints, drawing deductions from their presence and their characteristics. Others go further and use the lines on the palm of the hand or the marks made by mice in the sand as a means of prognostication. Divination in its wide range of forms is probably a feature of all human societies, though it has become less central to decision making in the West over the last four hundred years. It usually involves the interpretation of visual signs, not those made by humans but those specifically independent of them. Other signs, including those on Ojibway birch-bark scrolls, are made by humans and are usually intentional, aiming to communicate to other persons. These serve as mnemonics; they do not systematically represent and develop speech forms in the way that a fully fledged system of writing does, enabling man to express in writing all (and at times more, but also at times less) than he can in speech. Such systems of writing, according to our view, were a major breakthrough that differentiates human cultures in significant ways.

The work that I began in connection with Ian Watt (Goody and Watt 1963) and continued in various studies has been part of a cross-disciplinary effort to study the effects of writing on social organization and cognitive processes by a number of scholars from different fields: cultural historians of the ancient and medieval worlds, psychologists, anthropologists, classicists, specialists in literature, even linguists and philosophers (Goody 1968, 1977a, 1986, 1987). That has paralleled the work done on the advent of printing and its importance not only in the West (Eisenstein 1979; McLuhan 1962; Ong 1974) but also in the East (Pelliot 1953; Rawski 1979). While not all contributors have been in perfect accord, there has been general agreement that the advent of writing was of primary importance in the history of human cultures.

I want to discuss some of the particular objections raised by Street (1984) to my general argument, then look at the problem discussed by John Parry (1984), Christopher Fuller (1984), and John Smith (1984) concerning the fixity of oral works and the malleability of written ones with reference to India, and finally examine some data on Egypt (Baines 1983) more as confirmation than as criticism.

I do not think Street has altogether understood our use, albeit loose, of the term *restricted* in relation to literacy. Watt and I employed it in three ways: first, in relation to systems of writing that do not utilize the full technical possibilities of, for example, an alphabetic system; second, to indicate those systems in which literacy was used in restricted rather than general contexts, for example, predominantly in religious settings; and third, where literacy was restricted to specific social groups or individuals. Street claims that to describe early Islamic or Christian literacy as restricted is to indicate that people are "closed off from alternatives" (Street 1984: 142). From one standpoint I would agree; otherwise why refer to Islamic or Christian literacy at all if it does not imply some ideological closure? In the larger perspective of written cultures we saw writing as opening up alternatives; that was the thesis of our original paper. The restriction has to do with potentialities. If one chooses to teach children only in a language that is not their mother tongue (and does not approximate to it), whether Arabic in West Africa, Sanskrit in India, or Latin in Europe, the situation can reasonably be described as one of restricted literacy. Learners have to acquire another language (often a dead one) before they can add the skills of reading and writing, which obviously requires more time and effort than learning to read in the vernacular. Such demands often result from the close connection between literacy and religion, the aim of educators being to make accessible sacred texts written in the classical language (though there are certainly secular forms of this literate conservatism). Alternatives are doubtless opened up by such learning, but certainly fewer than if the text had been translated and writing taught in the vernacular.

Street's misunderstanding of the argument is made plain at the end of his book. Commenting upon a similarity he perceives between Bernstein's work on language codes and the model of literacy in which its consequences are autonomous, he notes that some researchers have attempted to find in literate cultures not only "relative culture-specific skills and styles" but also "the 'deeper' abilities such as 'abstraction' and 'logic.'" He goes on to remark that the supposed absence of these qualities "is bound to lead to judgements of inferiority and would, indeed, call a person's very humanity into question." The language is extravagant and hardly does justice to either the intelligence or the humanity of those on whom he comments. When Watt and I discuss the relationship between logic and abstraction and the use of language (written language), we are not referring to general qualities underlying humanity. We are concerned with two specific aspects of the problem: first, with what lay behind the general contentions of writers such as the French philosopher Lucien Lévy-Bruhl (concerning logic) and the anthropologist Claude Lévi-Strauss (concerning the abstract) on the differences between types of society that they variously describe as primitive and advanced, hot and cold, without any necessary implication of differential evaluation of human attributes (at least in the latter's case, the concrete being valued as highly as the abstract); second, with giving specific meaning to the notion of "logic" in the restricted sense of certain cognitive operations (especially the syllogism) practiced by the Greeks and others. In this (technical) sense it is as absurd to say that anthropologists have discovered "logic" in all cultures (Street 1984: 225) as it would be to suggest that logic in the wider everyday use of the word (which I use without quotation marks) could ever be absent. Despite constant insistence upon this point, it is obvious that some readers (distracted, perhaps, by earlier, often universalistic arguments against Lévy-Bruhl) have not grasped the point. Whether this is their inability to "read" (that is, to distinguish the different uses of the word *logic*) or our inability to communicate, I do not know. The same problem occurs with the notion of "abstraction." Of course one is not implying that any group of language users displays an inability to make abstract statements. Nor is one decrying the concreteness of oral language, which in poetic discourse is strongly valued. One is talking about specific features of relative difference, which may have (sometimes loosely) been described in these terms. Street himself gives many examples of the comparative decontextualization of written language—for example, as a national medium, which must make it less appropriate at a more local level. The obvious point is made by Street himself when he says:

> All who use language do in fact engage in abstraction and, as anthropologists have demonstrated, "logic" is to be found in all cultures, accounts of its absence in specific groups being due simply to misunderstanding on the part of travellers and observers from alien cultures. (Street 1984: 225)

However, the rules of "logic" (in the formal sense, attached to the practice of logicians) are not found everywhere, as L. S. Vygotsky and Aleksandr Luria showed for Central Asia (Scribner and Cole 1981). It could be argued—and is a frequently held position of anthropologists—that all logics differ by culture. It could also be claimed that they differ by subgroup and even by individual. Yet we often perceive general elements that enable us to talk about the logic of a particular group. Following the same line of thought, the point Watt and I made is that the formal logical operations involved in the development of the Aristotelian notion of contradiction, of arguments such as the *modus tollens* or of the explicit notion of the syllogism, were critically dependent on the introduction of writing. Street himself describes how William Labov showed that youths labeled illogical "turned out to be perfectly logical and intelligent once the tester had learnt to understand these cultural rules and conventions" (Street 1984: 225). That is the point we are making—that the "intelligence" of the tests is (as Meyer Fortes, Ruth Benedict, and many others pointed out fifty years ago) a function of the questions and the questionnaires. But we argue that the difference is not simply cultural in the purely relativist sense. Of course there are individual differences among societies as well as among individuals. But we also perceive some general differences (and by *general* we do not necessarily mean universal; a statistical likelihood is sufficient to support our argument against the random distribution that the purely relativist viewpoint would imply) within a certain range of societies associated with the advent of writing. Our interpretation of any particular feature may be too strong; on the other hand, some implications may have been overlooked. Neither possibility weakens the general thrust of our argument.

One further problem lies in the differences we perceive in the notion of "cause." Street writes of Iran:

> While the reasons for the success of villages such as Cheshnmeh can be explained in terms of the institutional factors that I have cited, particularly in contrast with plains villages during the same period, I would also like to consider the extent to which a certain knowledge of, and acquaintance with, specific literacy practices was significant. The factors I have already considered make it clear that there is no one determinant to which the changes described can be reduced and the arguments put forward throughout this book weigh against any attempt to ascribe causal significance to "literacy." (Street 1984: 171)

He can now consider, he asserts, with "less grandiose ambition just what significance literacy practices might have" (Street 1984: 171).

I myself see no little difference between Street's attempt to "explain," or find significance, and mine; no one can possibly ascribe one determinant to any human situation, except perhaps in some very simple cases. So the problem must arise at the level of causation. Street, like others, appears to view this notion as deterministic in relation to a single factor. But many investigators in a variety of fields of scholarship understand causal factors to be plural in kind, as in the sort of causal model prepared by Wright and others (see Goody 1976); of course, such models require a weighting of the factors involved, and this can be done only where an individual is not merely asserting the role (or the primacy) of one or more factors but making some attempt to assess these against each other. Optimally this assessment involves numbers; this is not easy to manage with much of the material treated by social scientists and especially anthropologists, but it is what they often attempt to do in a very rough way by allocating primacy, dominance, or subdominance to various factors in a particular social situation.

However, we must distinguish the analysis of a particular social situation, such as Street is undertaking in his study of an Iranian village, with another perfectly reputable form of social inquiry, namely, the attempt to examine the influence of one or more factors (for example, the means and modes of production, communication, destruction, and so on) upon social life, either in a particular context or in a general one. It was the latter enterprise that Watt and I attempted with regard to alphabetic literacy. In essence the enterprise is no different from T. S. Eliot's suggested inquiry into the influence of the steam engine on the rhythms of modern poetry, or Elizabeth Eisenstein's comprehensive investigation of the influence (also seen as consequences or implications) of printing on social life (1979). Indeed, the background of Watt's and my essay lay partly in our wartime experiences of being virtually without (printed) books over a long period; our previous, almost total reliance on the materials for reading and writing was driven home to us. But that understanding also derived from the line of inquiry embodied in Q. D. Leavis's *Fiction and the Reading Public* (1932), which later influenced Watt's own important 1957 work, *The Rise of the Novel*. Here Watt considered, among other things, the ways in which printing and the consequent change in the reading public (consequent not in the sense of necessarily following but of printing being a prerequisite both to the growth of education and to the mass production of the book) influenced the rise of the genre. Whether or not Watt was right in every respect (and the position has been argued by Michael McKeon [1987], among others) is neither here nor there. What he did not do at that time (nor did we subsequently, in relation to writing) was to propose a theory of single-factor determination for the rise of the novel. In the case of writing we were attempting, like Eisenstein, to investigate its "implications" (Goody 1968a) and especially to see how its introduction could better account for some of the differences that many perceived between "primitive" and "advanced" human societies, between oral and written cultures.

That this was not a binary theory but an attempt to account for binary theories was stated in the first paragraph of the paper Watt and I wrote together. To put it in its simplest terms, we saw different scripts as having different implications (which in turn were influenced by social factors), and we saw block printing, the rotary press, and so on each as having further implications for systems of communication and social life more generally. So too, of course, did different types of reading (silent, aloud), systems of punctuation, and suchlike, all of which we mentioned but which were dealt with more fully by Watt.[1] The alphabetic system was one of many changes in the system of communication, but the one whose influence we were examining, just as Street at one point singles out the influence of orchards as a system of production on social organization (1984).[2] But if instead of examining a particular social situation, one chooses to study sharecropping, the jury system, cargo cults, or the wheelbarrow, one is not proposing an "autonomous" theory, as opposed to an "ideological" one. The investigation is starting from a different point of departure. This topic-oriented focus is not an approach that many contemporary anthropologists adopt because of their overriding preoccupation with understanding specific field situations in the round, but it is a perfectly legitimate type of undertaking, one that was common enough earlier on, is still central to many fields, and remains key to certain anthropological inquiries, such as Sidney Mintz's study of sugar in *Sweetness and Power* (1985). Unfortunately, if seen from the fieldworker's position (which is normally one of "porridge functionalism," where everything influences everything else in an unspecified way), it looks like an investigation that assumes autonomy, single-factor causal paths, determinism, even materialism and all those other ills that modern Marxists warn us against. The inquiry into the influence of any factor (for example, of language on human social life) cannot be understood by creating "ideal types" of theory (which the author admits no individual holds) and then knocking down the autonomous straw men that have been created.

Malleability and Fixity of Traditions

I turn now to discuss some particular problems that have been raised in the comparison between text and utterance, and between written and oral cultures, that is, cultures with and without writing.

Some authors (for example, Parry [1984] and Street [1984]) have sought to query statements about the immutability of texts by pointing out that Hindu gurus engage in reinterpretations of the written word; Street claims that "the mullahs, like the gurus in India, had scope in

practice to say what they like" (1984: 137). While such extreme vol-
untarism does not correspond to my limited experience with either
gurus or mullahs, I have never for one moment confused text and interpretation.[3] In saying that a text is relatively unchanging, I am making
the simple point that Watt and I made in 1963 when we quoted Yeats's
comment about Genesis: "There would be no Darwin had there been
no Book of Genesis" (Hone 1942: 405).

On the other hand, I do not accept Street's overly functionalist view
that the meaning of the text depends entirely on how one learns to interpret it. One feature of a text, as distinct from an utterance, is that
people can return to it for support of particular attitudes or practices;
as one example, some Anabaptists or Mormons have gone back to the
Old Testament to find a textual basis for polygyny, which runs very
much against the prevailing ideology or culture. In such cases the text
is in effect modifying the ideology or culture rather than the other way
around. The return to earlier Islamic premises by the Khomeini regime
in Iran (and fundamentalism more generally) represents another example. But in any case the text of the Qur'an remains effectively invi-
olate, while many Christians still worry about the assertion of a virgin
birth presented in a text that is now some two thousand years old.

I will try to put the problem in another way. Fredrik Barth has noted,
and attempted interestingly to account for, the enormous variations in
myth and ritual that obtain among adjacent societies in New Guinea
(1987). I have been faced with the same problems in northern Ghana,
where although one can discern many of the same building blocks in
adjacent cultures, there is constantly emerging variation in a single myth
(such as the Bagre of the LoDagaa) and, perhaps to a lesser extent, in
ritual. What strikes even the most superficial observer in India and East
Asia is the extent of the common core, despite all local variation. A
look at the superb statuary from Southeast Asia in the Musée Guimet
in Paris will make one realize there is no problem identifying Hindu
deities and their associated myths that have endured not unchanged,
not uninterpreted, but in recognizably similar forms over the generations. Partly this is a question of iconography, which can be as persist-
ent as writing and for the same material reasons; the whole relationship
of iconography to other forms of graphic communication (especially

writing) is one that needs to be explored (Goody 1987; Baines 1983). Of course, there is some malleability of written traditions; but we referred to the enduring nature of texts, not traditions. Texts that cannot simply be "disposed of," like earlier versions of an oral recitation, encourage commentaries, often written, sometimes oral. But the point is that X's written commentary on Y's text takes on a quality different from that of verbal comments on a seminar paper, since it has a different audience in time and space, becomes part of a quasi-permanent corpus of argument that is therefore in one sense cumulative, and tends to take a shape other than that found in purely oral cultures (a point to which I will later return). Malleable all traditions necessarily are; but malleability takes different forms and different speeds, and is in any case domain-specific. One kind of cumulative malleability depends on "library" storage, on reviews of the "literature." It is unhelpful to state, as Street does, that I would associate "a particular development of malleability" only with an oral tradition (Street 1984: 138). Written traditions, as distinct from texts, are certainly not immutable. However, to identify the "fixity" of Islamic scholars with that of oral poets (Street 1984: 138) is to misunderstand the nature of that activity. The mutability of sacred traditions, whether oral or written, is unlikely to be disputed, but to ignore the different implications of changes in modes of communication for text and utterance, which are also modes of storage, is to put one's head too deep in the relativist sand. That is not for one moment to imply that text entirely replaces utterance; means of communication are cumulative rather than replacements. I certainly do not think, as Street seems to suggest, that the literate channel replaces the oral in literate societies. It modifies the oral, yes, but does not replace it, except perhaps for some scholars who sit all day in their dim libraries and look at life in general through their short-distance lenses.

When we speak of "changes in cognition," in modes of thought, as one of the implications of literacy, we are not thinking of a point at which the introduction of writing suddenly changed the totality of man's understanding of the universe. That would involve a notion of "instant literacy," immediate changes in ways of life and thought following the introduction of writing. In the first place, early writing (and a significant part of later writing) was restricted in various ways: in terms of persons, either because of the nature of the script or because of hierarchical constraints, and in terms of subject, because of largely religious control of the uses of writing. Hence the potential consequences of any change were also restricted. Second, as John Baines (1983) has emphasized for Egypt and others have done more radically for Mesopotamia (for example, Schmandt-Besserat 1993), the development of scripts was a gradual process, meaning again that the implications were not fully realized at once. Third, cognitive techniques and practices that one might possibly attribute to writing—certain forms of argument, such as *modus tollens,* or the writing of "history" from records—are themselves subject to long-term developments, partly the result of internal factors and partly because of external factors. History in Greece begins with genealogies and chronicles, leads into the more narrative forms of Herodotus, and develops stricter notions of evidence with Thucydides. Such a progression holds for written knowledge more generally. Fourth, and most important, the "logics" of written cultures, even advanced ones, do not represent a complete break with those of simpler societies. The differences—for example, in the written development of syllogistic usage—are often small in themselves, representing not so much a major shift in cognitive manipulation as an opening up of possibilities for further exploration. The appearance of such "logics" is not necessarily a sign of a quantum jump in logical operations, nor of course does it represent the discovery of logical thinking in any global sense. But "logical" procedures, in the limited sense in which these words are understood by philosophers, logicians, and linguists (and indicated here, as with "history," by the use of quotation marks), are composed of a series of such activities that appear to owe their initial formulation as formal operations to the presence of writing. This does not mean that analogous, less developed forms of procedure such as opposition, polarity, and contradiction are not present in societies without writing, nor yet that the formal versions, once developed, cannot then be fed back into such cultures. The interface between the oral and the written is always a complex matter.

Our discussion depends upon distinguishing between societies (or cultures) with and without writing or other literate techniques (and of course the extent of literacy and the content of texts in the former), as well as between the written and oral traditions in societies with writing, and again between literate, nonliterate, and illiterate individuals.

This is to use the word *tradition,* defined close to its roots as a "handing over," in the sense of intergenerational communication, indirect as well as direct. It implies some notion of quasi continuity, if only over a single generation. There is a more limited way in which the word is used to cover the literary tradition or its oral counterpart, consisting of folktales, legends, songs, riddles, and proverbs—what I have called "standardized oral forms" in order to avoid some of the possibly distorting ambiguities that may arise when using the term *literature* (that is, having to do with letters). While there is no hard-and-fast line to be drawn between the verbal art forms of societies with and without writing, certain genres, such as the novel (or in music the symphony), are clearly products of the former alone.

Not only do the genres differ, but even some of those that are universal change their characteristics over time. A written work necessarily has a beginning, a middle, and an end. An oral composition may be added to at any time and by different people. The notion of unity, so central a feature of post-Aristotelian literary criticism, is much less useful in examining an oral product. What one hears on a particular occasion is less likely to be the product of a single human mind at a single point in time than it would be with a literary work. The notion of the individual signature at the bottom of the canvas is out of place when the mural has been touched and retouched by numerous hands in the course of its preparation.

Smith has made a parallel objection to Albert Lord's "oral theory," referring to a northern Indian epic that is formulaic and thematic, yet consists, he claims, of a fixed text. Consequently he places more emphasis on memory, indeed on the possibility of verbatim repetition, in oral performance than do Lord and others, myself included.

Smith's discussion brings up an important matter of interpretation. Lord characterized the oral epic as "composition during performance." In his examination of the Rajasthani epic of Pabuji, Smith finds that two performers, one year apart, produced "versions of an 11–12 hour epic that were 'identical,'" the differences being limited "to the level of singing 'ho' in one performance and 'ha' in the other, or using two different words meaning 'king'" (1966: 55). Even different singers over time "sang what was in essence the same text. Divergences were naturally greater between two pairs of performers than between two performances by a single pair, but even so the similarities were far more striking than the dissimilarities." By this he means that in two performances with unrelated singers, 23 percent of the text sung was held identically in common, 18 percent was equivalent, and 36 percent consisted of formulae known to both sets of performers, though used at this point only by one. Only 23 percent, he claims, could be said to be truly unique to one or the other performance. On the other hand, only another 23 percent was truly in common.

Smith argues on this basis that "the text of the Pabuji epic is memorized verbatim by its singers," though it is not learned by heart (the difference being based on a distinction between memorization through habituation and memorization by deliberate effort). The use of the phrase "memorized verbatim" raises interesting problems. Smith has recorded one feature of the reproduction of utterance that we noted in analyzing the extensive material on the Bagre of the LoDagaa of West Africa, namely, that there is relative stability in the versions of one individual but much greater variation in the versions of different individuals (Goody and Duly 1981; Goody 1972). The difference is surely that between recall and memory. If one is thinking of the stability of a text over time, then what matters are the differences in transmission between different singers. And if it is the case that we find only 23 percent held in common between related singers (Smith 1966: 56), then one can hardly speak of verbatim memory as distinct from recall. The consequences for the epic itself are considerable, and under these conditions one may legitimately doubt whether we can posit a common text across performers. Of course, the narrative outline may be similar; narratives (as well as accounts of rituals, which have an external point of reference) are more likely to resemble one another than the kind of speculative discourse that marks the Black Bagre (Goody 1962). This is the point Lord is making when he writes that the singer "builds his performance on the stable skeleton of narrative" (1964: 99), and it appears to be similar to Smith's own contention that the singer learns by heart not the entire text but "all major occurrences of the story, and all obligatory formulae; performance consists of recalling and matching these." Naturally enough, any given singer will accomplish this in much the same way whenever he performs (Smith 1966: 57–58). Any given singer, yes, but different singers, no. What each man stores in memory differs from the next, at least to the tune of 23 percent, which is surprisingly large in view of the fact that this is a narrative sung by a professional group. But whatever the extent of the variation, it is evident that in this second case we are dealing in degrees of difference that are plainly of another order than those found in versions of written texts, even when these are transmitted by mouth.

Clearly I do not mean that writing in itself stifles invention in general. That would be quite contrary to its overall effect. But such consideration does occur in the field of religion, where the words of the gods are held sacred. Fuller himself makes a comment on writing as a conservative force:

> Goody (1968: 14–15) suggests that religious texts tend to have a conservative function, because orthodoxy in ritual or dogma is considerably preserved by adherence to authoritative texts. In fact, as we can see, the Āgamas lack this function; indeed, they have now become tools in the hands of reformists, as attention is drawn to the gap between practice and Āgamic precept. Such a role is surely common for sacred texts in all literate, world religions. (Fuller 1984: 209)

Any disagreement here is a matter of the words we use, for I have myself made precisely the same point about back-to-the-Book movements in Islam and Christianity. Watt and I stressed this aspect of writing in relation to myths and genealogies, that is, the gap that develops between practice and precept in authoritative utterance, where, for example, current moral norms or current social relations have undergone changes subsequent to the book having been written (Goody and Watt 1963; Goody 1968). In terms of religious texts, a realization of this gap may produce one of the following: a return to the Book of the kind I have discussed elsewhere, an imaginative allegorical reinterpretation, an open recognition of the gap (as is the case, I would suggest, with the usual Christian view of the Old Testament or the Hindu view of the oldest Vedas), or a relegation of the actual text itself to a category of the unread (which is perhaps effectively the same thing). But each of these eventualities, the comparative frequency of which it would be interesting to ascertain, depends upon the fact that a statement about, for example, ritual practice has been conserved in writing even when views have changed.

Conservation is not the same as conservativeness, but it is an essential prerequisite. If written statements are to be aligned with changes in current thinking and still accepted as authoritative, they have to be deliberately changed, re-formed, rather than undergo the more homeostatic adaptation that prevails in oral cultures.

The relation between text and ritual is clearly stated by Fuller: "All Siva temples in south India are, in theory, governed by the corpus of Āgamic texts. In principle, therefore, the rituals ought to be prescribed by a more or less uniform set of Āgamic rules," which are "the ultimate source of legitimate authority" (1984: 134).

The Āgamic texts are believed to contain the god Siva's "eternally valid directions for his worship in his own temples" (Fuller 1984: 135). There are said to be twenty-eight fundamental Āgamas, the oldest of which are believed to date from the third to the seventh centuries C.E. All were written in Sanskrit, including the commentaries and the manuals (from the eleventh century) that deal especially with the rituals, providing "explanations and instructions on ritual by systematising the Āgamas' directions and eliminating some of their inconsistencies" (Fuller 1984: 136).

In the Minaksi Temple of Madurai, the priests recognize the text known as Kāmikōgama as being authoritative. However, this literature is largely "unknown," and Fuller heard of only three priests in southern Tamil Nadu who were thought to be proficient in it.

> One . . . acquired much of his knowledge from his father, from whom he also inherited a large collection of Āgamic books and manuscripts. He knows Sanskrit and has committed to memory in the traditional manner large parts of many texts. (Fuller 1984: 137)

The second also inherited texts from his father and, with the encouragement of a local monastery, founded a school *(pàthasālā),* of which there are a handful in Tamil Nadu, for the sons of hereditary priests.

> The organisation of the school and the method of teaching is [*sic*] almost entirely traditional. The pupils have to obey the *guru* without question and they have to show him proper respect, for example, by prostrating themselves before him at the end of each lesson. (Fuller 1984: 137)

The pupils are also instructed, by other teachers, in Vedic and Tamil texts; they

> mainly learn by memorising exactly the passages recited to them by their teachers. It is considered vital that these passages' words, pronunciation and scansion are all memorised absolutely accurately, and this cannot be done by reading books. This again is the classical pattern; "in the ancient education system of India," writes Kane (2: 327), there was a "great prejudice against learning from books" and exact renditions of texts "could be learnt only by oral instruction." Only when a passage has been fully memorised does the teacher explain its meaning. (Fuller 1984: 138)

The course lasted six years, during which time the students learned to recite passages from the major Āgamas and from a ritual manual. How much they understood was difficult to assess. The guru himself thought he could give the boys only a general idea of the overall Āgamic scheme and some practical instruction in the rituals; complete training would take a further six years.

Criticizing the ignorance of the priests, reformers of various kinds have regarded schooling in Āgamic literature as a way of improving the present unsatisfactory situation. It is Fuller's point that education would not meet these hopes, partly because of the difficulties of mastering the relevant material and partly because while everyone acknowledges these texts as authoritative, they do not provide the expected guidance for the running of the temples, for "neither the Āgamas nor the ritual manuals actually contain the kind of explicit liturgical instructions that priests and others commonly suppose them to contain" (1984: 139–40). First, as in the preparation for the worship of Siva, the texts prescribe certain steps that would take too much time to carry out. Second, many details of temple worship cannot be found in the texts. Hence Fuller insists on the wide gap between practice and precept.

Writing was linked to the whole system of support for the temple. The Minaksi Temple was maintained by two types of benefaction, which Fuller refers to as endowment lands and land grants to officiants (1984: 92–93). Public worship is supported by a multitude of these endowments, each of which provides the materials and meets the cost of specified rituals or segments of them. Originally the donor would alienate his share of the produce of an area of land; many endowments appear to have been established by kings, their ministers, or their relatives, but some were created by monasteries, wealthy families, caste associations, and the like, although not all these were in land. Each such endowment was controlled by its own trustees and managers, over whom the temple had little control. However, since 1800 it is the administration of Minaksi Temple (not the priests) that has controlled a considerable number of such endowments (often taken over on the grounds of mismanagement), and centralization has continued apace.

Land grants (*inām,* abolished with compensation in 1949 and 1964) were also made to officiants. These were originally tax-free but later were taxed lightly for the benefit of the temples themselves; in other words, the officiants were entitled to the king's share of the land revenue, the tax collected in grain or cash by local agents from the assigned villages. A priest continued to have a right to such benefits only if he performed public worship at the temple. Such rights were inherited in the usual way, along with the duties; they could also be transferred, along with the duties, to others. Since independence, these land grants have been abolished, reducing a potent source of conflict. The priests still receive a cash income, but the greater part now comes from the gifts of worshipers, as has long been the case in northern India (Fuller 1984: 92–98).

I wrote earlier of the promotion of cultural activities by means of the written word. Clearly an interest in the past is characteristic of all human societies, but the existence of written documents makes possible different modes of analysis of what has gone before. What we meant by attempting to explain the contrast between history and prehistory is neatly illustrated by Baines's account of literacy in ancient Egypt.

> Later Egyptians, and Egyptologists, define the dynastic period, which began . . . perhaps a century after the first writing, as the be-

> ginning of history. . . . Written records of the names of regnal years
> were introduced then. These "annals" name the years by events
> that show a conception of the king's historical role . . . expressed in
> caption-like phrases, not texts. Enumerative, chronological lists of
> them developed with writing itself. . . . "History" is thus set off
> from "prehistory" by an ordering process. (Baines 1983: 576)

As he points out, "history" does not at this stage imply a discursive interest in the past, still less an analytical one. On the other hand, the basis for such a development is being laid, for one cannot proceed to
the discursive and analytical without a method of accumulating and
comparing annals. A simple kind of record can exist in oral cultures;
in drum histories of the kind found in the West African kingdom of
Dagomba (and more cryptically in Gonja), events are linked to the
reigns of specific monarchs, and the same is true of the often somewhat
fuller stool histories of Asante, where knowledge is transmitted through
the king's Spokesman.[4] But the difference between these oral records
and literate annals is immediately apparent when we look at the Gonja
or Kano chronicles, which are not simply examples of a West African
tradition of historiography but display a more general feature of many
early historical records (Goody 1954; Wilks et al. 1986; E. Goody,
forthcoming).

In Egypt, among the first types of text to emerge by the end of the
Old Kingdom, around 2150 B.C.E., were "copies of legal decrees and
proceedings and important private contracts, which could be displayed
in order to make their terms public and operative in perpetuity" (Baines
1983: 577). Gradually ethical precepts, which were connected to the
avoidance of litigation, came to be recorded. In later times, apart from
monumental versions of legal documents and the written court proceedings of the Old Kingdom, "one finds the use of documents as overriding evidence . . . , the citation of precedent and of statute . . . and
a law code. . . . Elaborate record storage served legal institutions. . . .
Legal matters could be 'published' in monumental form in a protected
but accessible place" (Baines 1983: 589). Baines sees these practices
as largely responding to needs that can be differently catered to in a
nonliterate society, but "they acquired a notable rigour and generated
new modes of intercourse, as in a subject's right to petition the king in

writing" and in the creation of wills (technically deeds of delayed transfer, which included wills by and for women). Wills may have reduced
conflict where there was a loose rule of inheritance or, conversely, allowed just such flexibility to exist. All this is certainly true, but when
we consider the institutions of even such a legally conscious but nonliterate state as that of the Barotse of Zambia (Gluckman 1955b, 1965),
some of the general differences between these and written law, such as
the use of precedent and even the concept of norms, are related to the
employment of writing for legal purposes. And clearly of some general
cognitive significance, important for concepts of "truth," are the type
of "publication," the perpetuity of contracts, and the overriding importance given to written over oral evidence.

In Egypt there is evidence for schools at the end of the third millennium B.C.E. In later periods reading and writing were learned by copying, and probably reciting, classical literary texts. Traditional texts
were transmitted for millennia, and from the New Kingdom on (1550
B.C.E.), this transmission probably occurred in the "house of life," a
scriptorium attached to temples, where the texts were also studied in
depth. It is interesting to note the importance of copying and possibly
of reciting, that is, of internalizing written texts in precise form. Where
the latter happens—and this is the case in Islam and in India, as well
as with much Bible reading in the West—verbatim memory becomes a
more important factor (though now irrelevant from a strictly functional
point of view) than in oral cultures, so that those features that facili-
tate this process (for example, metrical form and formulaic construction) may play a greater part in early written productions than in oral
ones. I would suggest that an appreciation of this situation does something to account for the discrepancies that some have perceived in the
thesis of Lord and Parry (Lord 1964; Parry 1984; Goody 1977a; Smith
1966; Baines 1983). Also, such scriptoria become yet more important
"when written and spoken language had diverged a long way, and its
position in society will have narrowed access to elite culture further
than previously, contributing to later images of Egypt as a land dominated by priests" (Baines 1983: 581). Hierarchical or scholarly divergences of linguistic usage are not unknown in oral societies, but writing
adds a new dimension by creating whole "dead" languages that refuse

to die (in oral societies they are truly dead) and giving rise to a new axis of hierarchical (class) differentiation based on knowledge of the texts. Moreover, with the accumulation of texts over time, the discrepancy between the language of ancient texts and current written practice grows, bringing with it the need for "scholarship" if these earlier texts are still to remain part of the contemporary repertoire. The disparity between the written text and some oral utterances was of course present from the beginning, even if we assume exact transcription without any transformation. Baines notes that the texts give no expression to dialects, though we know they always existed (1983: 581). Written languages have to select one of many speech forms to establish as the standard. The consequences are important: "The standardized written form aided communication over the country, but must have been for many at best half-way to a foreign language" (Baines 1983: 581). Whatever the feedback of writing on patterns of speech, this discrepancy remains a fundamental handicap in literate education, especially for children who have not had access, through their families, to speech that approximates more closely to the written form.

Literacy became essential in Egypt for the proper performance of temple ritual; that involved a lector priest, literally "he who carries the festal (papyrus) roll," who was also, according to Baines, a magical practitioner (1983: 585). Temples were centers not only for schools but for scholastic activity more generally, as they became repositories of written knowledge, the language of which diverged more and more with time from that of ordinary speech, leading to the need for deliberate reforms rather than for the constant homeostatic adaptation characteristic of oral cultures (Baines 1983: 584).

While there was no emergence in ancient Egypt of a canonical religious literature accompanied by exegesis, in the form in which we know it from Judaic or Christian tradition, the copying and glossing of traditional Egyptian texts were institutionalized; these processes are not identical, but both involve written procedures. The existence of those procedures has profoundly transformed the course of human life.

The concepts we use abound in ambiguities and depend upon the interests of the particular scholar. Clearly memory, in the sense of mental storage, is critical in all cultures and in most situations, even in those cultures that have developed and instituted external memory banks (books, computers, paintings, stained-glass windows, and the like). So too is oral activity—oral discourse, of course, but also oral composition, performance, and tradition (this last, again, in the literal sense of "handing over"). If I am interested in the general comparison of how writing can influence cultures, I am concerned with comparing the artistic and other productions of cultures that are purely oral (in the sense of not having writing) and those that utilize the written channel in various ways and in various contexts, giving rise perhaps to restricted literacy. Hence to refer to this basic schema as binary, as a great-divide theory, as is done by Finnegan (1973), for example, seems to me a fundamental misunderstanding. Even in our original article, Watt and I were attempting to explain (not advocate) the binary division that exists in many folk and scholarly (especially anthropological) views of the universe. We were looking at this supposed dichotomy in terms of changes in the means of communication, assuming that these were multiple. Indeed, Watt's original work had to do with the effect of printing on the rise of the novel, part of a topic discussed more generally by McLuhan (1962) and in a more scholarly way by Eisenstein (1979). What we were saying then, and continue to maintain, is that some aspects of differences or changes (that is, the differences seen in a dynamic or processual frame) that are widely perceived and often attributed to the *Geisteswissenschaft* of the culture or to the genius of a people are more reasonably associated with differences (changes) in the means and modes of communication. The traditional characterization of these general differences is a matter for question; the dichotomizing view sees the concrete posed against the abstract, the hot against the cold, the primitive against the advanced, the traditional against the modern. Those dichotomies are unacceptable as they stand; so too are those that counterpose myth and history, logic and alogic (or perhaps intuition). But the traditional characterizations were nevertheless pointing to some overall differences in cognition, in the understanding of and approach to the world, that are related to the ways in which communication takes place. If we are more specific and deal, for example, with the proportion of nouns to verbs in text and utterance, respectively, we encounter a domain in which writing is more abstract than speech.

Such observations do not necessarily mean that we cannot, for example, find relatively decontextualized lists in oral cultures (not to mention the speech acts of members of written cultures), let alone an interest in the past, rationality, and so on. They mean only that certain aspects of the cultural activity so described are promoted by and transformed by the written word.

The development of communication is obviously not simply a matter of adding a new channel, since that addition alters the nature and especially the content of existing channels. Oral communication (orality) in societies with writing is not the same as in those without. Equally, while in complex societies one may well find subcultures whose members communicate only in speech (and it has been estimated that twenty-seven million Americans are virtually unable, unwilling, or unmotivated to do anything else), comparisons of those subcultures with oral cultures in the fuller sense have to be treated with great caution. A nonliterate is not the same as an illiterate, though they may have various points in common.

As a consequence, a so-called oral tradition that supplements a written tradition cannot be thought of as the same as the oral tradition in a society without writing. In the first place, the latter has to bear all the burden of cultural transmission, whereas in the Yugoslavia of the 1930s (the time focused on in the well-known research of Parry and Lord) or in the Germany of the 1800s (the time of the brothers Grimm) the oral tradition was vested with only part of the total body of literary activity, of standardized verbal forms. The café songs of Novi Pazar and the fairy stories of the European countryside formed part of popular culture, which was supplemented by printed romances and other works linked to the literary-based manifestations of high culture that emanated from the towns. And while these aspects of popular culture may be formally related to the productions of nonliterate societies, both their role and their content have clearly undergone important changes. From the standpoint of the total society, their role is now subordinate to those of written origin, although they are differently valued by different social groups and at different points in the life cycle; fairy tales always tend to be for children, even of the upper and literate classes. Nevertheless, a certain regrading has taken place in their content. Since religious practices and beliefs are largely based on scriptures and in the hands of literate priests, what is left in the oral tradition tends to be magic rather than religion, the peripheral rather than the core. In other words, the content of the oral tradition tends to be marginalized.

Part of the process of transmission between the generations is what we call "education," referring to the deliberate act of teaching the young, usually in separate organizations such as schools, colleges, and universities. In oral cultures learning is inevitably a more contextualized process, taking place on the job rather than in a special setting. Verbal accounts of acts and beliefs are little used compared with what happens in their written equivalents in literate cultures; there the medium in any case permits a more abstract, more generalized, more analytical approach. Oral learning entails a greater amount of showing, of participation. Hence the world of childhood is less segregated from that of adults. Children sit or play around when discussions and performances are taking place, absorbing at least the general atmosphere of these activities and occasionally, if they listen attentively, some of their content as well. Much more learning takes place publicly, since verbal communication depends upon the voice, upon face-to-face interaction. Whereas in literate cultures an individual can go off by himself with a book, in oral cultures a partner is needed as narrator or instructor. Partly for this reason in oral cultures the act of being alone, communicating to oneself, is sometimes regarded with suspicion, as possibly a prelude to some malicious action such as witchcraft or sorcery. Solitary activities such as eating alone may take on a negative value; in this sense, the privacy of the individual is not necessarily prized, since the interactive nature of human life is more immediately represented to the actors.

In other words, what Durkheim saw as the mechanical solidarity of simpler societies is not only a matter of the division of labor. Social relations and values have more obviously to be upheld in face-to-face situations; there is no possible recourse to a text as an external source of guidance. It is the same with the very meaning of words. Semantic properties are validated in interaction; past meanings cannot be recalled by historical etymology; that which is not carried in memory has disappeared for good. The restriction of linguistic communication to the oral channel accounts for some of those features that are commonly regarded as characteristic of the "primitive mentality." The greater concreteness and relative lack of abstraction must be linked to the dominance of the context of the interactive situation. Inhibitions are placed on the elaboration of general rules, which are more often implicit than explicit. In the terminology developed by Max Weber and Talcott Parsons, such societies tend to be particularistic rather than universalistic.

Social institutions are much affected by the limitations of the oral channel. Religions tend to have a more local focus, to be more clearly intertwined with everyday life. Legal procedures are less governed by general laws, by formal procedures. Precedent will rarely play a distinct part in lawmaking, since recent judgments constitute the practice of the law itself. There are few written formulations that outlive their usefulness and turn into an embarrassing relic for the judge to modify and the legislature to undo by formal resolution. The homeostatic tendencies of memory usually consign to oblivion what is no longer wanted. Oral communication in the political field obviously restricts the buildup of bureaucratic government. While it does not prevent the rise of states, the relationship between the center and the periphery is likely to remain a weak link in the chain of messages. Both internal communication and central accounting can operate by adding mnemonic devices to oral storage, but the more complex the organization of the state and the economy, the greater the pressure toward the graphic representation of speech.

2
Memory in Oral Tradition

I n approaching this topic, I decided first to consider the question of memory in oral cultures, which is what I call those without writing. In fact, the phrase "oral tradition" is also used to refer to what is transmitted orally in literate cultures. The two forms of transmission are often conflated, as in the well-known research of Parry and Lord on the Yugoslav epics, from which in my view they draw the wrong conclusions about the Homeric poems being created in an oral culture. Both Homer's work and the Yugoslav epics, like most epics, are products of early literate cultures even if they are performed orally. Oral performance in literate societies is undoubtedly influenced, to different degrees, by the presence of writing and should not be identified with the products of purely oral cultures. The point is not merely academic, for it affects our understanding of much early literature and literary techniques, which are seen by many as marked by the so-called oral style. To push the point to a speculative level—speculative since I do not know a sufficient number of unwritten languages (and here translations are of no help whatsoever)—many of the techniques we think of as oral, such as the assonance of Beowulf (or of Gerald Manley Hopkins), the mnemonic structure of the Rig Veda, the formulaic composition of the Greeks, and even the very pervasive use of rhyme, seem to be rare in cultures without writing. In his book *Primitive Song*, C. M. Bowra sees a metrical structure in such cultures as being required by the nature of the song, but there is "nothing that can be called metre in the sense of having a regular number of strong beats, determined either by loudness or by the time it takes to pronounce a syllable" (1962: 85). Repetition is present, he writes, but alliteration and rhyme are incidental if not quite accidental ornaments, used very intermittently. Greenway, too, asserts that rhyme is rare in "primitive literature" (1964: 122), and while Finnegan disputes this judgment, she does agree that "it is probably among oral literatures in close contact with writing that full vowel and consonant rhyme is most significant. It occurs in late Latin songs, modern English nursery rhymes, and the rhymes of the troubadours, British ballads, Malay *pantun* quatrains and Irish political songs," as well as in medieval Chinese ballads (1977: 96; see also Finnegan 1970).

So these features are more characteristic of oral performance in literate cultures, where word-for-word memorizing and recall become highly valued (that characteristic is critical), than of the more flexible traditions I have encountered in purely oral cultures. Let me elaborate on this important difference.

Communication in oral cultures takes place overwhelmingly in face-to-face situations. Basically information is stored in the memory, in the mind. Without writing there is virtually no storage of information outside the human brain and hence no communication over great distances and long periods of time.

Plato decided that writing would ruin the memory and that oral man remembered much better than his literate counterparts. From that time on we often hear tales of the phenomenal feats of memory in such cultures, of remembrancers who recall the complexities of tribal histories or of bards who recite long myths or epics.

Those tales have continued to be told. The American sociologist David Riesman (1956) claimed that members of oral cultures must have had good memories just because nothing could be written down. That common assumption was made even by Frederic Bartlett, author of the well-known book *Remembering* (1932) and friend of the great psychologist-anthropologist W. H. R. Rivers, when he claimed that nonliterate Africans had a special facility for low-level "rote representation" (Neisser 1982: 16). It is true that such societies are largely dependent on internal memory for transmitting culture, for the handing down of knowledge and customs from one generation to the next. However, not everything is memorized in a perfect form, that is, verbatim.[1] I have known many people quite unable to give a consecutive account of the complex sequence of funeral or initiation rites; nevertheless, when the ceremonies actually start, one act leads to another until all is done. One person's recollection will help another. Moreover, a sequence such as a burial has a logic of its own. At times visual clues may jog the memory, as when an individual is trying to find his way from one place to another; one clue leads to the next as in a paper chase.

However, observers who are more critical, such as Scribner and Cole in their work among the Vai of Liberia (1981), have found rather poor verbatim memories in oral cultures and have concluded that this is a result of the lack of the general mnemonic skills and strategies that come with literacy and schooling. That is to say, nonliterates performed badly in standard psychological memory experiments (Cole, Gay, Glick, and Sharp 1971).

But what are these standard tests measuring? In the psychologists' terms, memory means exact, verbatim recall. You give somebody a list or a series of objects, remove the list, and later ask him to name the items, giving points for the right sequence or for simply remembering the items in any order.

But is that the type of memory that oral cultures really employ? It is true that some information has to be held in memory store in an exact (or more or less exact) form. I could not communicate with you by words unless we had similar lexicons. That is a prerequisite of social life, the basis of which is acquired early on in life; children are mimetic. But what about adults, for example, learning lists of objects or words? I do not doubt there may be some occasions on which a member of an oral culture might find it useful to be able to recall items in an exact way (a list of trees, for example), but from my own experience they are very few and far between. It is simply not a skill of any great value to them; that value comes with schooling that decontextualizes knowledge to form lists.

Many experiences are placed in memory store, but most of these we do not absolutely need to keep in any precise form. Indeed, in oral cultures the notion of verbatim recall is hard to grasp. I mean partly that in the African languages with which I have worked I do not know a word for the memory (though there is a verb referring to the action of remembering, which in LoDagaa is the word *tiera,* "to think," or alternatively *bong,* "to know"—the concepts are not differentiated). Everything that is learned goes into memory store in some form or other, at first by a process of imitation that enables us to acquire a particular language so that we can communicate in the cultural context in which we find ourselves. Humans may already have the general inbuilt ability to learn languages, but we need imitative learning to enable us to acquire exactly, precisely, verbatim, the basic features of a specific language. That imitative faculty, which seems to be an attribute of apes and men but not of monkeys, is subject to fading; our ability to acquire new languages diminishes rapidly after puberty. Younger children, on the other hand, acquire exact knowledge with ease; think of the ability of young boys to remember the model numbers of cars or engines, then think of your own.

All cultural knowledge in oral cultures is stored in the mind largely because there is little alternative. When we congratulate the members of oral cultures on their good memories, at one level we are simply saying that they have no other storage option, such as the books that we ourselves can pull down from our library shelves and consult to find the reference for a quote we vaguely remember, or to discover the name of a bird we did not know.

What is clear is that much of this oral knowledge is not stored in the precise way we think of in literate cultures when we talk of memory. In fact, nonliterates are often in exactly that state of having a vague recollection in their heads and of being unable to take down a book to do what we do. Hence they may just have to create new knowledge or new variants to fill the gap.

There are some exceptions to this dependence on internal memory in the form of visual mnemonics. However, mnemonics serve only to jog the internal memory; they are no substitute for it, unlike a book or a computer. These mnemonics are material objects and sometimes graphic signs that fall short of fully fledged writing because they do not record linguistic expressions per se but only loosely refer to them.

We should be quite clear about the difference between a mnemonic system (or memory) in oral cultures and the kind of recall that full writing permits and encourages. At one level they may be seen as equivalent, especially to Derrida and other postmodernists, anxious to stress the relativity of cultures and, in effect, the lack of hierarchical (evolutionary) difference. That position neglects cultural history, for culture does have some developmental sequence in which changes in the modes of communication are as important as those in the modes of production. The information stored in mnemonic systems is rarely verbatim, word for word; instead such systems present you with an object or a grapheme to remind you of an event or a recitation, which you then elaborate. It is true that if I recite a short tale and offer you a mnemonic, you may be able to repeat it almost exactly. But such reproduction depends upon my telling you the tale and showing you the mnemonic. No one else can read the tale directly off the object. There is with mnemonics no precise distance communication as there is with writing, where we have a fixed, societywide code that enables us to establish more or less perfect linguistic communication over distance in time and space with people we may never have met but who have learned the code.

You can do quite a lot with visual mnemonics. Morphologically, these precede writing, which is a code rather than a mnemonic. While the latter are important for many purposes, they have a very different role to play. Visual guides to territory (a kind of map) are said to be provided by the sacred *tchuringa* of the Australian Aborigines, which offer the new initiate a stylized picture of the local territory that he can then use in the walkabout he has to make at puberty, which introduces him not only to his local environment, both practically and symbolically, but to kin and neighbors in the surrounding area.

Take another case, that of the Spokesman attached to the Asante court. Apart from knowing "custom" in a general sense, he acts as a remembrancer in a more specific one. He is the one who knows the history of the chiefdom's stool, or throne, which he recounts on ceremonial occasions. Its history is largely a dynastic one, and of this he is reminded by the blackened stool that each king leaves behind as an ancestral shrine to which sacrifices can be made. Associated with the stool may be various objects linked to events that took place during the reign of that king. Together with the marks on the shrine, including the remnants of the sacrifices that have been performed there, these objects give the Spokesman mnemonic clues about the history itself. Items fastened to the state drums may perform a similar role. "Among the 'insignia' of the Golden Stool of the Ashanti," wrote the anthropologist-administrator R. S. Rattray, were "iron and gold fetters, gold death-masks of great captains and generals whom the Ashanti had slain in battle since the time of Osai Tutu," the founder of the dynasty. "Among these were likenesses of Ntim Gyakari, King of Denkyira; Adinkira, King of Gyaman; Bra Kwante, King of Akyem; and Mankata" (Rattray 1927: 130–31). The last name refers to Sir Charles M'Carthy, the British general who was killed by the Asante at the battle of Esamanko in 1824 and whose skull decorated the shrine.

Some of these histories are not so much memories as attempts to influence the present audience regarding aspects of the ownership of land or the extent of jurisdiction. In his account of his inquiries in Asante, Rattray speaks of the great difficulty of getting at the truth. Even formal recitations are influenced by contemporary concerns. The divisional history of Asumegya, as given by him, begins with the first chief, who came out of the ground on a Monday night followed by seven men, seven women, a leopard, and a dog. The seven pairs of humans plus the chief of the Aduana clan almost certainly represent the eight matrilineal clans, or *abusua,* that lie at the basis of Asante kinship and social organization. It is their present existence that prompted the history, not, of course, memory itself. The first king was followed directly by one in whose time the Asante threw off the yoke of Denkyira and became independent; that is, it jumps straight to the seventeenth century. The doings of later kings in such histories may be recalled by objects or skulls attached to the stool or the state drums.

Among the Luba of southeastern Zaire, genealogies are traced back to founding ancestors. While we may consider these as myth, the Luba see them as truthful; "present events are legitimized by their relationship to the sacred past, as enshrined in the charters for kingship. . . . These charters were sacred, to be guarded and disseminated by an association called Mbudye. Mbudye historians were rigorously trained 'men of memory' who could recite genealogies, lists of kings and all of the episodes in the founding for kingship. Mbudye adepts created rituals for memory transmission in the eighteenth and nineteenth centuries, when the Luba kingdom was at its height" (Phillips 1995: 285). They also invented mnemonic devices to assist historical recitation (Reefe 1977). Nevertheless, the genealogies, like most examples of that oral genre, often reflected present interests rather than past facts.

Principal among these devices was the *lukasa,* a hand-held wooden object studded with beads and pins or covered with incised or carved symbols. In the catalogue of the 1995–96 exhibition of African art at the Royal Academy of Arts in London, the boards are said "to still serve as mnemonic devices, eliciting historical knowledge through their forms and iconography. Through oral narration and ritual performance, insignia serve both to conserve social values and to generate new values and interpretations of the past, as well as to effect general and political needs." During Mbudye rituals to induct rulers into office, a *lukasa* is used to teach the sacred lore about culture heroes, clan migration, and the introduction of sacred rules; it also suggests the spatial positioning of activities and offices within the kingdom or in a royal compound. "Each *lukasa* elicits some or all of this information, but the narration in fact varies with the knowledge and oratorical skill of the reader" (Phillips 1995: 285). That variation is critical.

Luba memory devices, then, did not preserve thought or store language so much as stimulate them. They offered a multiplicity of meanings through their multireferential iconography. Colored beads, for example, referred to specific culture heroes, lines of beads to migrations. They also encrypted "historical information about genealogies and lists of clans and kings. Yet the reading of these visual 'texts' varies from one occasion to the next, depending on the contingencies of local politics, and demonstrates that there is not an absolute or collective memory of Luba kingship but many memories and many histories" (Phillips 1995: 285).

Graphics, drawings that have made part of the journey to writing, may serve a similar purpose. In his account of the birch-bark scrolls of the Ojibway of Canada, Selwyn Dewdney explores the question of how in one particular form of shamanism, what he calls "tutorial shamanism," the teacher's version of a myth is prompted by a series of drawings that map out, for example, the journey of a hero or the migration of a clan, and indicate the events that happened on the way (1975). These graphics are not writing in the full sense of the word. They serve as a mnemonic, and no two interpreters will give altogether the same interpretation, even if they have learned from the same master at the same time, so that the divergence between one version and another is of quite a different order than we find with two readers of the same linguistic text.

I want to point up a paradox (perhaps a misconception) about memory in oral cultures and in the oral component of literate ones, the contrast I raised at the outset. In Jewish tradition, the Mishna is the oral law, as opposed to the Mikra, the written law. The oral law was delivered by God to Moses with the Pentateuch, but as an oral supplement. It now exists in written form but is learned verbatim, so that it is in a sense preserved orally in memory (and if necessary transmitted by word of mouth). The word *Mishna* is in fact derived from the verb meaning "to teach," especially "to teach by means of oral repetition." Indeed, "the Mishna on Idolatry" is described as "apparently arranged with a view to facilitating the process of memorizing the contents." Some digressions "are really mnemonic aids based on the principle of association of ideas." What is strange here is that at the very period in time when literacy made it possible to minimize memory storage, human society adopted the opposite tack, at least in some contexts. As the editor of one published edition of the Mishna writes, "It is a point of curious interest to the modern mind that the great mass of knowledge and opinion . . . was retained in the schools for the most part, perhaps entirely, without the aid of writing. It was transmitted by memory alone, through the process of oral repetition, whence indeed came the title 'Oral Tradition'" (Edwards 1911: xvi). But it is significant that the people in charge of this process were the scribes *(soferim),* the experts in writing themselves.

The role of the scribes shows that this editor's account is not wholly adequate. Students may hear a spoken version of a literate text and store that in memory. For example, many people learn the Lord's Prayer in just this way, because fully knowing a text can mean learning it by heart, but there is always a written version to check back with. Some people, especially fundamentalists, still set themselves the task of learning the whole Bible by heart; more frequently the same is done for the Qur'an. Indeed, Muslim schools are often entirely directed to this very end; in non-Arabic-speaking countries, the Qur'an continues to be read and learned in the original language (literally the words of God), which means that many simply know the sound of the text by heart without knowing Arabic or how to read it. If some students also know part of the meaning, it is because they have learned a parallel text (or possibly an utterance) at the same time, not because they can translate from one language to the other or understand the text on its own. That form of learning leads to the development of verbatim memory skills. When they tested these qualities among the Vai of Liberia, Scribner and Cole found that Muslim literates, even if they could not understand Arabic, were more proficient than those literate in English or in Vai itself, and more proficient than those who knew no script at all.

A similar situation seems to have occurred in the famous case of the Rig Veda. We often hear about the way this text has been transmitted orally from one senior generation of Brahmans to the next. Note that once again it is the scribes who are in charge of so-called oral transmission—in itself an indicative fact, for we know that the text had been available in written form since the fourteenth century, and indeed some scholars have suggested it originated a thousand years earlier, in 150 B.C.E. or even 500 B.C.E. (Goody 1987: 112). The Rig Veda contains many internal mnemonic devices (as does the Mishna) in the form of the tight phonetic structure of the verses, which seems to depend on alphabetic literacy and helps the learner to recall exactly the content. It is always possible for the teacher to look back at the text and check to see that he or his pupils are not making a mistake. This form of transmission is associated with the fact that the Brahmanical tradition asserts that the Vedas were *apauruṣeya*, produced by no human agency: They existed eternally and before the world itself (Goldman 1991: x). So for them there is no original written text composed either by God or by man. Other Brahmanical textual traditions trace their origins to superhuman seers, or *ṛṣis*, who, like the Vedic seers, had, at least by implication, "access to similarly unconditioned texts that lend the tradition an aura of inerrancy" (Goldman 1991: x).

Similar considerations perhaps apply to the works of Homer, about which there has also been a long controversy as to whether or not they were composed in an oral culture. What is certain is that they were communicated by recitation to the audience at the annual Great Dionysia. On the other hand, they already existed in written form, having been composed or transcribed around 650 B.C.E.; their communication was in the hands of reciters *(rhapsodes)* rather than those of lyric poets or composers *(aoidoi)*.

Why should people who could read from the Bible, the Qur'an, the Rig Veda, or Homer commit those works to memory and then produce them as spoken language? Partly because, as I have mentioned, "knowing" a text often means memorizing it word for word; internalizing the meaning with the words means that those words become part of you, integral to your consciousness, and may be helpful in organizing your experience. Another factor is that being able to quote in this way from, say, *King Lear* is prestigious (showing you are an educated, possibly self-educated, man or woman); also, memorization is often necessary in turning a text into a performance (as with a play onstage) for broadcasting purposes. And to speak the words of the gods is especially charismatic.

Of what significance is the difference between oral communication of an internalized (written) text and an utterance in a culture without writing? As members of a written culture, we tend to read our own memory processes onto oral cultures, looking at them through literate eyes, whereas we need to try to look at them from within. Consider the difference. If I hear a longish poem or recitation in an oral culture, I can try to place it in memory store and later repeat it. The original reciter may even correct my repetition in an attempt to reproduce his own version. That procedure may lead me to assume that exact reproduction is the aim and end of this learning, a procedure that in this context allows little room for invention and creation. But leaving aside the intention of the actors, which is often uncertain, is it even theoretically possible to reproduce perfectly a recitation of any length in an oral culture? Remember Bartlett's experiments where he sat people in a circle and, starting at one point, asked for a short verbal message to be passed from one individual to the next, unheard by the others. The message at the end of the process was quite different from that at the beginning

(Bartlett 1932). So the answer to the question is that exact reproduction of long recitations in purely oral cultures is very difficult indeed. When the teacher is absent, you have nothing to refer back to, no book, no model, except the sounds that remain in your memory. We know how fallacious that can be. For reasons possibly connected with Freud's discussion in *The Psychopathology of Everyday Life,* you may consistently transpose a name, for example, from "Mr. Brown" to "Mr. Black." If the teacher is absent and there is no fixed text, you pass on this change to all who hear you. The transmission between you and your audience is as it was between you and your teacher, that is, privileged; the recited version becomes the truth, becomes orthodoxy; you are the holder of "proper speech," as the LoDagaa would say. You become the authority, albeit temporarily.

Let me give you a specific example of what happens in an oral culture with which I have worked for many years. I have already referred to the Bagre myth of the LoDagaa of northern Ghana, which was part of the initiation rites of an association that provided medical and other benefits. I first recorded this recitation in 1950. The association was secret and I was not a member. But a former resident of the village, called Benima, who had converted to Islam and now lived in a nearby stranger's settlement, or *zongo,* understood my interest and offered to recite the myth to me as it had been taught to him by his father's brother, Naapii. Over the ten days he recited, I wrote down his every word and got some partial explanations of the contents in a rough translation. I was partly convinced by what Benima said and others hinted at (and by the analysis of myth by many anthropologists such as Claude Lévi-Strauss and Bronislaw Malinowski) that we were dealing with a fixed recitation that people knew by heart and that was handed down in more or less exact form, as a unique cultural expression, from generation to generation. Had this been true, it would have been a fine example of exact memory in oral cultures. And indeed, I was told how some new initiates who showed promise would be taught by an elder and their recital would be corrected by him.

I could not at the time easily test this assertion of fixity, for it was before the days of portable tape recorders.[2] But nevertheless, I should have known better, partly because I had earlier used the work of Bartlett in discussing the difference between oral and literate cultures (Goody and Watt 1963), and partly because embedded within the Bagre that I had written down (and which was eventually published by the Clarendon Press in 1972) was an encouragement to the neophytes to go to the performances of other groups or lodges, even of different branches of the association, and learn how they recited. In other words, variations were acknowledged and in a sense encouraged. The implications ran contrary to much current thinking. The whole view of myth in oral cultures has suffered from the fact that until recently we usually had only one version of any long recitation (already a considerable achievement to take down), which looked (and was discussed) as though it were a fixed, unique feature of that culture that should be analyzed in a timeless way. If another version was recorded, the corpus was still treated as finite, with variants as simply homologous alternatives of the same basic structure, as in the case of literary texts.

Some twenty years later, in the 1970s, I returned to that village as well as to neighboring ones to make further recordings with my collaborator and coauthor, Kum Gandah, who, as a member of the association, could attend the actual ceremonies. By now portable tape recorders had become available and we could record a number of versions on the spot and then transcribe and translate them later on at our leisure. The whole task was a long one, spread over several years, but we completed some fifteen versions of the White Bagre (the first part of the recitation, which was closely tied to the ritual performance and which acted as a mnemonic, a prompt) and nine of the Black Bagre (the second part, much more speculative, even philosophical, dealing with the acquisition of culture by mankind as well as solutions to his troubles).[3]

The differences between the versions were large. They were significant even when the same man recited on different occasions and greater still when different men recited on the same occasion (for the myth had to be recited three times at each ceremony). Between nearby settlements (for example, Birifu and Lawra, ten miles apart) they are enormous. In table 1 I give the variations of the White Bagre in length only.

The differences between versions not only obviously have to do with length, with whether some incidents have been included or excluded, but also are of a transformative, generative kind. Some stress the role

Table 1. Length of Recitation of the White Bagre

Version (recitor, date when known, occasion)	Number of lines
1. Benima, 1951, dictated	6,133
2. Nyin, 1969, Bagre Bells	3,917
3. Sielo, 1969, Bagre Bells (incomplete)	2,778+
4. Nimidem and Sielo, 1969, chief's house	3,940
4a. Nimidem, 1969	1,704
4b. Sielo, 1969	2,236
5. Kob, 1969, chief's house, leading to the Black Bagre	2,267
6. Sielo, 1974, in the open space in Beating of the Malt	2,239
7. Gbaa-Ziem, 1974, Beating of the Malt	1,260
8. Sielo, 1974, at the house in Beating of the Malt	2,225
9. At Gomble, 1974, Bagre Dance (Birifu, as all above)	1,204
10. At Yikpee, Lawra, first lineage, Bagre Dance, day two, morning of the Bagre Morning	(a) 24
	(b) 165
	(c) 84
11. At Yikpee, Lawra, second lineage, Bagre Dance	(a) 86
	(b) 114
	(c) 525

of God as the creator of man's culture; others emphasize the role of the intermediaries, the beings of the wild (or fairies), while yet others highlight man's own contribution to his culture (Goody 1996). Some are highly theocentric; others stress the role of different agencies. Nevertheless, the LoDagaa will often assert the unity of the Bagre, that all versions are "the same" (*boyen,* meaning "one"). That is because all are performed in the course of the Bagre rites; it is like saying that Evensong is the same whatever is included, different anthems, different prayers. But there is also another factor, for with oral versions recited at different times and places, you cannot easily make a comparison, not the way you can when you lay the written versions of Evensong side by side and actually examine particular passages. In the memory (as distinct from in the archive) the versions tend to merge into one another.

What happens in the learning process is that the neophytes undergoing initiation into the Bagre sit patiently through these lengthy performances, and those that show some talent as potential Speakers learn the mode of recitation, the recitativo, so that they can fit any thought or sentence into the loose rhythmic structure of the verse. They listen, learn (without exactly memorizing), and then when called upon give a performance of their own, retaining many incidents from those they have heard but omitting some and elaborating others.

Even what I initially regarded as essential incidents do not appear in other versions. In the first, dictated version of the Black Bagre there was an account of one of the original human beings crossing a river, which formed the boundary between this world and the next. Reaching the other side in a boat, he met with an old man smoking a pipe, who was God himself. As a result of an invitation, the human climbed up to heaven with the aid of the Spider, whose web served as a ladder. There he was shown how God created a male child. In the next version we recorded, some twenty years later, the whole of this incident, which at that time seemed to me structurally of the greatest importance, had been compressed into a few lines, which only I could now fill out. God now played a very different role in the whole recitation (Goody and Gandah 1981).

So depending on which version you select, the analysis will vary greatly. And there is consequently much less close a fit between myth and other aspects of culture (including ritual) than many functionalists and structuralists have suggested.

The indeterminancy is pervasive. There is a section at the beginning of each recitation consisting of some ten lines that I have called the Invocation. In the first published version it runs as follows:[4]

The Invocation to the White Bagre

Gods,
ancestors,
guardians,
beings of the wild,
the leather bottles [*which hold the divining cowries*]
say we should perform,
because of the scorpion's sting,
because of suicide,
aches in the belly,
pains in the head.

Even when I had given up the idea that the Bagre was fixed, I still believed this Invocation to be rigid, because people would confidently begin to speak these lines, and then an elder would correct a younger man's version; it is as if I were reciting the Lord's Prayer and someone told me, "No, not 'hallowed be *your* name' but 'hallowed be *thy* name.'" However, I have now recorded some dozen versions of these lines, and none of them is precisely, word for word, the same as any other. If an elder corrects a recital, it is on the basis of his own memorized version, his personalized model, which differs slightly from that of others. Since there is no fixed text from which to correct, variation is constantly creeping in, partly due to forgetting, partly due perhaps to unconscious attempts at improvement, adjustment, creation.

When you come to think of it, much cultural transmission has to be of this kind. It is a mistake to view the handing down of culture as the exact counterpart of genetic transmission, a kind of cultural mimesis; genetic reproduction is largely self-replicating, but human learning involves generative processes—"learning to learn," in Bruner's phrase. Some changes in the corpus take place because of pressures from the outside, forcing or encouraging adjustment, others because of deliberately creative acts that have little to do with adjustments of this kind; that you can see by examining neighboring cultures, as Barth does for New Guinea (1987), cultures that presumably must have once been the same. The LoDagaa area consists of neighboring settlements and of constituent lineages, each of which displays a number of differences from the others. LoDagaa "culture" is marked off from others only in a relative way, not by hard-and-fast boundaries. In fact, customary behavior changes gradually over a large region, like the dialects of a language. Dialects change because memory—mimesis, imitation—is imperfect; forgetting may occur, but in many cases perfect reproduction is not even aimed at. That is the same with other features of human cultures. In the absence of centralized mechanisms of control that inhibit change, differences in behavior constantly emerge in this way; there is little of the precise replication involved in verbatim memory.

Oral memory is, of course, simply experience reworked. Only in the light of such a notion can we account for the fact that neighboring oral cultures, even very small ones, display considerable differences and that the world offers us such great diversity, even among the simplest societies. It is written cultures, like written languages, that more easily manage to establish relatively stable internal norms over large areas that in certain spheres inhibit but do not altogether prevent diversity. It is only in literate cultures such as those of Cambridge Colleges that we find people reciting the same prayer every evening of the week, whatever the weather, whatever the national events, without any thought of innovation. It is also the case that in other spheres writing encourages diversity; examples are the high degree of turnover in the artistic world and the increased speed of the accumulation of knowledge. But in some ritual situations writing establishes a conformity, an orthodoxy, as with Religions of the Book, which endure unchanged over the centuries. Think, for example, of China, consisting of a fifth of the world's population. There one finds very similar marriage or funeral rites stretching from the far northeast right down to the southwest. Why? Because diversity of practice was deliberately suppressed by a civilizing process that introduced the Chinese script to tribal peoples. With the advent of schools came books on ritual that prescribed exactly how one should act on a variety of occasions. It was the duty of all citizens of the empire to follow these written rules and so to marry in a certain way. The written word sets up a situation that would be almost impossible in oral cultures, where storage is less exact and there is more room for the continuous creation of rituals (but less for the cumulation of knowledge that literacy provides).

I do not mean to imply that in oral cultures people are incapable of exact reproduction from memory store. As we have seen, mimesis has to occur for children to be able to learn a particular language, a process in which there is little room for imprecise reproduction. That continues to be the case with other bits of communication, including short events such as proverbs and songs (where the rhythms help). It also occurs with short narrative sequences such as those found in folktales. These undergo less transformation than the Bagre (indeed, some are incorporated in the Bagre, where they constitute relatively constant elements in the recitations; this is true in the works of Homer as well). Hence perhaps the broad similarity of many themes and shapes of folktales from culture to culture. But with longer oral forms, memorizing becomes more difficult and possibly less essential in the eyes of the people themselves. As I have indicated, it is really with literacy and schooling that the task of having to exactly recall vast quantities of data (often half uncomprehendingly) is seen as necessary to keep the culture going. It is interesting that the very earliest schools that taught writing, in Mesopotamia, required the pupils to read on one side of a clay tablet, then turn it over and write out what they had read on the other side. In other words, even though the advent of writing had provided a storage system that did not require one to memorize, schools insisted upon verbatim memory, as if, anticipating Platonic fears, they distrusted what the new medium would do to our mental processes. For certain limited purposes, such mimetic memorizing is necessary and advantageous. If you memorize the completely arbitrary order of the letters of the Roman alphabet, which does not even group together vowels and consonants and which goes back to a Semitic protoalphabet of 1500 B.C.E., you have immense control over the information contained in a telephone directory, a street map, or the index of any book in any language using the Roman script. You will have more difficulty in Russia and will be lost in Japan. But within the orbit of the same script, you will manage to find the address and phone number of a resident in a strange town. To do this requires exact learning of a totally arbitrary kind. So too does much of the advancement of science (as in the periodic table of elements or in chemical formulas), which depend upon exact internalization of less arbitrary forms of knowledge, since we may need to bring together different elements of information to solve a problem.

I have tried to refute a number of myths about memory in oral cultures. Verbatim recall is in general more difficult in such cultures than in written ones, partly because there is often no demand for word-for-word repetition of a recitation such as the Bagre. Every performance is also a creative act, and there is no distinct separation between performer and creator; that dichotomy does not exist, for, *pace* Derrida, there is no archive in oral cultures, at least not of the same kind as the United Kingdom's Public Record Office or the early libraries at Ebla or Alexandria. Of course, a greater part of culture is carried in the mind, especially language, but not always in a fixed archival way; hence dialects proliferate. Like all cultures, oral ones depend on stored knowledge, but much of this knowledge is stored in a way that makes it difficult to recall precisely, in the manner we usually relate to the psychological operation of memory. It is, as I have said, reworked experience. Marcel Jousse more or less identified memory with experience: "A man is only worth what he has memorized. . . . The memory is intelligence deepened. . . . The memory is the whole man and the whole man is memory" (Baron 1981: 100). Jousse had a particular thesis in mind. For him Jesus was visualized as the Rabbi Iéshona of Nazareth, who instructed his disciples in the Qehillâ, "*l'assemblée mémorisante*" where, using various techniques of what he called the oral style, the disciples memorized the words of the master in order to transmit them to the world at large (Baron 1981: 80). The problem is that the so-called oral style is a type of verbal discourse that characterizes a society with writing. The rabbis are nothing if not literate; their work is to memorize the written text, which they do by various mnemotechnical devices. In oral cultures one is less concerned with exact memory; on the other hand, this exactitude is important to Jousse, because if the disciples learned exactly by oral means, what has come down to us may be the precise words of Jesus rather than a version reconstructed by the disciples long afterward. However, the mnemonic techniques that he and others see as typical of oral discourse seem rather to be constructs of verbal communication in written cultures. That is possibly the case with Parry's formulas, with strict poetic structures of versification, and certainly with the kind of techniques used to memorize the Rig Veda. These appear to be not so much residues of oral cultures as the instruments of written ones. They are more frequently used in such a context because it is with literacy that the notion of exact verbatim reproduction becomes possible and valued. That is why such recall is associated with Brahmans and rabbis.

It is dangerous to speak of a collective memory in oral cultures; memory is held by individuals, who may have some elements in common. Here the danger is of falling into the earlier error of romantically inclined nineteenth-century scholars who oppose the communal composition of ballads to the individual creation of lyric poetry. The contrast is false, like other applications of this dichotomy; in this case it confuses composition, performance, and transmission. In oral societies each performance of a long poem such as the Bagre reshapes the work and (since performance is transmission) provides a new model for future versions. The process of composition, in the sense of the original act of creation, is impossible to reconstruct for lack of evidence or lack of relevance. On the other hand, it is in principle feasible to see how an individual has constructed his own performances, which tend to resemble one another more closely than the versions of different performers. Individuals contribute, some being more creative than others, but their signature rarely remains for long because of the very nature of oral transmission over time.

A further version of this collectivist fallacy recognizes the extent of variation but sees it as a departure from an "ideal" or underlying version. For example, influenced by structuralist approaches, Kellogg suggests that whereas written literature establishes communication between the minds of author and reader, the constant behind oral artistic activity is "an ideal performance, an aspect of tradition shared by performer and audience alike" (1973: 58): "As a written work remains in a kind of limbo until a reader picks it up and 'performs' it, so an oral work exists as an abstract body of rules and ideas until a performer embodies some of them in a performance." As an example of the latter, he refers to the Mwindo epic of the Congo, which exists as an unperformed and very long and detailed ideal (1973: 59). This and similar contentions represent a misapplication of the idea of a deep structure and share the same difficulties as those that viewed oral literature as emerging from the spirit of the folk by common authorship. While it is clear that in oral societies individuals play a different role with regard to verbal performances, we must be careful not to introduce the idea of unanalyzable processes or mechanisms to account for the differences.

The fact that virtually the only store of information is in the memories of men and women means that it is always susceptible to homeostatic transformation, to selective forgetting and remembering. There are, of course, techniques for preserving special kinds of information. But unless deliberately directed, memory bends to other interests, tending to set aside what does not fit. This feature of oral storage and transmission constitutes one aspect of the relatively homogeneous character of such cultures, in which uncomfortable dissonances tend to get overridden by the healing powers of oblivion while memory works with those experiences that link with others.

As a result, many individual inventions or personal doubts tend either to get set aside or else to be incorporated into the culture as if they had always been there. For example, innovations are a constant feature of religious activity, partly because of its creative complexity, partly because its solutions to practical problems of health and disease, of life and death, are usually inadequate. The God who failed is replaced by a new conception, or one imported from outside. Some of these creations are tried and rejected, while others live on, producing a changing constellation that, paradoxically, normally offers to itself and others the appearance of a fixed tradition.

To the actors the tradition may be regarded as the same over time, just as the versions of the Bagre are regarded by many as "the same." To interpret such statements as indications that each performance, each ritual, is a deviation from a disembodied ideal one is struggling to achieve, or that a hidden continuity lies at the level of deep structure (collective memory), has little justification in practice or in theory. Variations occur, some of them leading to significant change; otherwise how would one account for the extraordinary variety of oral cultures in relatively small areas such as New Guinea, the Amazon, or West Africa? Part of these introduced variations may be deliberately disregarded, part unintentionally so because the determination of verbal identity often presents difficulties. Since the long Bagre recitation of the LoDagaa has been written down, members of this society who can read are able to perceive that it differs over time and space from current versions. The version that was first written down gets invested with the authority of the ancestors who recited it, giving rise to the notion of an orthodox version from which others have strayed. But it might equally be maintained that in an oral culture the genuine version is that produced by one's contemporaries, not the oldest but the youngest, since this will reflect the influence of present interests rather than past concerns. Here as elsewhere, there can be no true orthodoxy without a "fixed text" of some kind or other, often arbitrary.

In the same way that change tends to get swallowed up by the nature of oral memory and the mode of oral transmission, so too do doubt and skepticism. Members of oral cultures certainly doubt from time to time the validity of their gods, their rituals, their premises. But only when these get written down does a real tradition of criticism emerge, a tradition that builds on itself. Incredulity, disbelief, is partly a matter of placing alternative versions side by side, of recording systematically the results of predictions, of perceiving in visual form the ambiguities of oracles. Partly, too, it results from tapping into a critical tradition, whereas in oral cultures the slate tends to get wiped clean for every generation, maintaining the appearance of homogeneity of belief, of total attachment to predominant cultural values.

But an oral culture is not held as a whole in everybody's memory store (except for language, which largely is). Memories vary, as does experience. Bits may be held by different people. Having partial recall, they prompt one another regarding what to do at a marriage, a funeral, or the Bagre and in so doing re-create cultural events anew. The notion of the static nature of oral cultures may, unlike our own, be partly true for the technological aspects. But for other features there is greater flexibility. It is literate societies that proliferate mnemonic devices, not only the verbal sort but also the spatial kind discussed by Frances Yates in her well-known book *The Art of Memory* (1966). The limitations of memory in oral cultures, the role of forgetting, and the generative use of language and gesture mean that human diversity is in a state of continuous creation, often cyclical rather than cumulative, even in the simplest of human societies.

3

The Construction of a Ritual Text:
The Shift from Oral to Written Channels

As an example of the shift from speech to writing, in this case discussing channels rather than cultures, I want to examine what happens when we represent in writing a ceremony we have witnessed in performance. It is often assumed that classical ritual texts, like recitations such as Homer's epics or the Vedas, went through a previous existence as utterances handed down from the immemorial past in largely the same form, and that these were simply transferred to the new channel when writing became available. I have argued elsewhere (1977b) that the process of writing down a myth tends to transform it on three levels—content, structure, and language itself—rather than simply transfer it to a different register. Judging by recent experience in West Africa, this transformation seems especially likely to occur when the actors themselves have written down the oral products of their own cultures; in trying to get at what they see as the heart of the matter, they have rarely limited themselves to the notion of exact transcription. But transformation occurred even when an outsider (such as an anthropologist) was trying to preserve the oral form as far as appeared possible, for prior to the advent of the tape recorder the literate observer had to resort to having people dictate long utterances well removed in time and space from the cultural performance itself. Many of these oral products were not even dictated but rather retold, summarized, and revised in the process in unauthorized ways and by unauthorized speakers. Effectively each method would tend to lead to changes, some more severe than others.

Here I want to extend the argument from myth to ritual, by which I mean ceremonial acts and the accompanying words as distinct from separable, marked recitations where action is set aside in favor of telling. With ritual the transformation is often much greater, since for the most part language cannot provide a direct record of the nonverbal acts and much of the verbal accompaniment does not consist of memorable speech, or speech to be remembered, in the same way as the recitations do.

I need to expand the comment on this use of the term *ritual,* a concept that I have discussed in earlier papers (1961, 1977c). Some writers have tended to use the word for nonverbal acts alone, a tendency that has been embodied in the myth/ritual dichotomy, whereby the former was conceived as the verbal counterpart of the latter. In what follows I am mainly concerned with the writing down or composition of discourse other than myth, rather than with the creation of a total score or handbook for such a performance.

Again, because the point is much misunderstood, I want to stress that I am comparing the products of oral and written cultures. The production of a written text by an author combines the use of the normally unspoken (oral) and the visual (written) word. The communication, or at least the performance, of a written text may involve silent reading to oneself, reading the text aloud to another, or even the use of the spoken word alone, as in the performance of a play where the actors have internalized the written word. But an actor may also learn a written part indirectly, that is, by listening to another person rather than by reading it himself. To take the process a step further, a person may compose a sonnet in his head, although few would consider the sonnet as anything but a literary form, made possible (like the novel) by writing. I do not mean to assert that all aspects of linguistic communication in written cultures are influenced, let alone determined, by writing or even by a variety of graphic representations. Nevertheless, many are, in a cognitive sense as well as a formal one; so too is much nonlinguistic action, from map reading to football strategy to the composition of a symphony. The same applies at a societal level. Even cultures without writing may be influenced by the products of written cultures—for example, by their religions of conversion. Features associated with the existence of a text may be transmitted to individuals and cultures that do not possess writing (Goody 1968b).

One further point of clarification. In referring to the sonnet, drama, novel, or symphony, I plainly do not mean that all lyric, dramatic, narrative, or orchestral composition is dependent upon graphic recording; rather, only certain subtypes are. In the case of the novel and the symphony this fact is too obvious to require comment. In that of the sonnet, I refer specifically to the tendency in written poetry to employ complex rhyming schemes in a formal shape, and in drama to the tendency for much written work deliberately to exploit not necessarily the Aristotelian unities but the constraints of the program for subsequent performance. In making this point I do not mean to assert that the art forms or genres of purely oral cultures have neither rhyme nor unity; instead, it is the particular type of rhyme or unity that is at stake, complicated in the first instance, formalized in the second.

Let me turn first of all to the task facing a scholar who is trying to provide an accurate written representation of a formal recitation or a ceremonial performance, that is, of myth or ritual. In attempting this for the Bagre performances or for the funeral ceremonies of the LoDagaa of northern Ghana, I would have to allow for informal as well as formal communication. Take linguistic action. A representation of either ceremony in writing would have to include not only the marked recitations, in which mystical (special) discourse is set off from ordinary (other) discourse, but also a great deal of speech activity, which, while not ordinary in content (that is to say, it is largely directed toward the carrying out of the ceremony), takes the form of everyday speech. A passage from the transcription of a recording of various speakers in the course of the Bagre ceremony will illustrate the point, including the shift from the less formal mode of imperative discourse to the most formal mode of authoritative recitation.[1]

The Lawra Bagre, 1974–75: The Bagre Dance
Day 2: Bagre Morning (the morning session), various people speaking

My friend!
It's my friend I am calling.

Why did you come here?
[*Indecipherable voices*]
Well, that one is finished,
That one is finished.
Eh! Napolo!
Napolo!
All of you listen.
You over there, listen.
Don't you see we're appealing for help?
The way I'm suffering is obvious.
Look, the next performance, is it the Bagre?
[*Indecipherable voices*]
The knowledgeable people aren't here.
That's what I'm saying, knowledgeable people aren't around.
Knowledgeable people aren't around,
that's how it is.
You sit down there and say there are no knowledgeable people, get up!
Get up!
Get up! Get up and stand by.
Women, get up!
Where are the women?
Divide yourselves into two groups and come and help us perform
    the Bagre.
Heh! you sitting there, come over here and go in between.
All you women,
all you women come in [*between the neophytes*].
The sun is rising high!
All you women,
heh, don't go that way.
All you women who don't want [*to be here*]
should return home.
Eh, indeed! You stranger women, stranger women,
keep out of the way, as I'm coming on that side.
Let's get on with the performance and stop [*talking*].
If you help in this, it will be the end.
Come and see how we are performing it.
[*Indecipherable voices*]
My friend, whom did you send?
To the Bagre?
All you women, see I've raised my left arm; listen to the recitation.
    When they finish and I put it down like this, you'll know it's over.
    Do you hear?

The women, are they ready?
They are ready!

The White Bagre [Invocation]

Earth shrine,
ancestors,
see the Bagre.
[When I speak, you should raise your hand and strike.]
God of the heavens,
see how I strike.
[Raise it and strike.]
Sorrow
takes hold
and bursts out
in boils,
bursts out
in the ruin
of childbirth,
in the ruin
of farming,
in the ruin
of hunting.
And they made them
toil away
all along,
pressing them,
pressing them persistently,
until they arrived
at last year,
suffering all the time.
The divination,
what did it say?
They will not
permit
this matter
to ruin us
and cause
[*so many*] deaths
in the old house,
[*destroying it*] completely.

In unmarked speech, anyone (or at least any senior man) can and does contribute or interrupt. The more marked the speech/recitation/song, the greater the degree of authoritative monopolization of communication; this may not necessarily take the form of monologue but may be a dialogue, either of choric question and answer or of statement and repetition, processes that are clearly associated with techniques of learning. However, except with very short compositions, the teacher himself is rarely seen as entirely infallible, despite this tendency to authoritative monopolization, since from time to time he may be subject to some correction by others of relatively equal status; but here such comments take place only when there is a pause in the proceedings. Some situations are obviously more impermeable to correction than others. You cannot interrupt the Bagre recitation, though rarely does it escape subsequent discussion among the participants about the fullness or fluency of the performance, both being assessments of comparative achievement. Such corrections are general in nature, since they refer not to a fixed text but to differing models in people's minds of what has to be done. Above all, instruction is not confined to the formal relationship between teacher (that is, Speaker, initiate) and learner (neophyte); the latter may learn by watching other performances, from his contemporaries, and from other participants at other times, as well as from his own attempts at recitation. In this way each individual constructs his own standardized oral form, his own model in the mind, different from others but one to which he tends to stick.

At the beginning of the session that we have transcribed, the organizers try to get the initiates and neophytes properly assembled and to see that the main actors are present, including the Speaker himself. There is also the question, during the course of a long, elaborate, and interrupted ritual that takes place over several days, of picking up the threads, of establishing what has already been done and what has to come next. At the beginning, the Speaker, Napolo, is called over and there is some discussion about what should follow.

Beginning with the phrase "All of you listen," the Speaker asks the audience of initiates to pay attention. Discussion continues, and there is the usual lament about the men of today not knowing enough, a statement that is not specific to the occasion but has its roots in the characteristic features of much transmission in oral cultures: The Speakers, even at the moment of creation, think of themselves as recovering the irrecoverable, the knowledge of their predecessors, the ancestors. The women aides are placed next to the initiates and attention is called to the fact that the recitation is about to take place, the Speaker raising and lowering his left arm to mark the beginning and the end of formal speech, during which period no interruptions will be possible. There are other markers of the recitation, such as physical features that distinguish the performance—the place, the crowd, the authorities, and so on—and linguistically the recitation itself is set off because it employs a rhythmic form of recitativo, the utterance being phrased in short bursts (lines as I transcribe them), each punctuated by beating a stick on a wooden object, hardly music but certainly not noise. But the whole ceremony includes both marked and unmarked speech, just as the content of the myth itself consists of a verbal commentary on why we should be performing the Bagre as well as an account of the series of component ceremonies.

Given this intermingling of formal and informal communication, what happens when we produce a (written) text of the speech component of the entire Bagre performance, not simply of the myth, the recitation, and leaving aside the problem of a script or notation for the nonverbal components? The same considerations apply to the recording of the funeral ceremonies in their linguistic and nonlinguistic aspects (Goody 1962). I spent a long time trying to create such a script and transcript, but in a time before portable tape recorders, with a still camera but no movie camera or camcorder, using observation and inquiry. The answer is that both I and my respondents singled out the formal aspects, they to talk about them and I to write them down. In other words, we tend to consider as "noise" the elements of informal communication. So if I were trying to reverse the process and reconstruct an actual ceremony as enacted from the written text, the script would represent a version of the whole proceedings that had been drastically cleaned up into some more orderly, less informal sequence. The fact that my respondents did the same emphasizes the point that in giving an account of a ceremony after it has happened, or in presenting an abstract model of something such as a funeral, the actors are carrying out a task similar but not identical to that of the person with the pen. To the differences I will return.

Second, the process of writing down inevitably tends to eliminate variation. When I wrote my account of funeral ceremonies, I did not base that presentation on a single observation alone. I attended funeral ceremonies of all and sundry over a two-year period, and I attempted to represent in words the differences between the funerals of old and young, male and female, married and single. I tried not to produce a single synthetic account but to include and then explain the major variations I had witnessed. Nevertheless, I did so only over a small area and over a short space of time, and in any case I had to construct a model performance in order to display the variation. If I were to assume that ritual never (or rarely) changes, either on the surface or at the level of deep structure, perhaps neither time nor space would matter. But both with funerals and with the Bagre, these elaborate rituals showed considerable variation, both temporal and geographic, some of which could be linked to other aspects of society (for example, variations depending upon the status and life history of the actor, his clan membership, and so on) but also others that could not be accounted for in this way. The differences between ceremonies in adjacent areas are often of this second variety, and while some may become diacritical features used to mark the boundaries of social groups (as with xylophones among the LoDagaa), the majority can perhaps be explained only in terms of the richness of mythical and ritual invention, as Barth (1987) has also concluded for New Guinea. In other words, regional variations derive (at least in part) from differences that have emerged over time in the course of performance, that is, through creative interpretation or simply by having to fill a gap.

I have evidence of verbal differentiation not only in the numerous tape recordings of the long Bagre myth (Goody 1972; Goody and Gandah 1981; Goody and Duly 1981) but also in the nature of funeral songs, which inevitably contain topical and hence more changeable material. As for rituals, since action in the funerals is connected with the past of the deceased, since there is a degree of mimetic representation of events in his life ("taking out the dream," say the LoDagaa), these performances must necessarily reflect changes in that life, whether these have to do with a decrease in wild game in the area surrounding the village or with the beginnings of wage labor in the mines. However, the influences of such social or environmental changes would not necessarily account for much by way of variation among adjacent settlements, since these are all likely to be affected in roughly similar ways. The variations we find result not so much from an entailment with other forms of social action but from a lack of it, from the relative autonomy of such activity from other aspects of the social and technical orders. Taking the technical order first, the variations in agricultural technique in adjacent areas are inevitably limited by what in comparative terms is the intrinsic nature of the means-ends relationship. Since one of the available criteria used to define religious, ceremonial, or ritual activity turns on the nonintrinsic character of these relationships, such action is in principle much less constrained; it is more open to man's creative performance, or at any rate allows invention to creep into the repertoire.

It is true that another characteristic of ceremonial activity is an element of formality, a feature that might appear to run counter to the assertion of its continuing malleability. Formality certainly restrains change in ritual (and in cultures without writing it is perhaps the main factor to do so). On the other hand, it does not prevent imaginative reconstruction from taking place, partly because of the nature of the process of transmission in oral societies, where verbatim memory of long sequences is rarely demanded and frequently impossible, at least for speech; visual performance (as in charades) is easier to reproduce than verbal forms unless deliberate mnemonics are introduced. In the virtual absence of means of recording other than by mental operations, identity as distinct from similarity is difficult to establish.

I have spoken of the formal/informal mix as well as the problem of recording variation. In the first instance my written text, like any verbal account, has eliminated the element of informality and concentrated on the formal; in the second it has eliminated variation and established a single fixed text. But the utterance has undergone further change as the result of being written down, establishing itself in the case of the Bagre as one authoritative version (although accidentally chosen for me by circumstance) among many oral ones, and in the case of the funerals as one enduring model derived from one point in time and space.

This process of transcription obviously does not prevent further changes in the rituals, but at least potentially it provides a fixed point of reference for the participants that, if endowed with the sanctity of ancient tradition, may continue to act as a possible model for future action, as an account that has to be taken into consideration. This is one way in which the written version differs from the oral. Let me cite an actual example. In northwest Ghana people have already begun to refer to written works on funerals and on the Bagre as sources of performance. It is the same elsewhere. Dr. Alex Kyeremateng told me that in preparing a pamphlet for the installation of the Asantehene in 1970 he had given great weight to the earlier published account of the colonial officer and anthropologist R. S. Rattray (1923). Particularly for complex, rarely performed events, the memory of old men was not in itself sufficient. Quite rapidly the text assumes authority over the utterance. Not that the written versions of the funeral ceremony and the Bagre have become the only accepted ones among the LoDagaa; they do not have the status of a handbook. As yet they play a very peripheral part and do little to inhibit oral reproduction. Yet one can see how a new orthodoxy can arise in precisely this way and come to dominate the alternative versions, just as the adoption of the Midlands speech for written English created an orthodox English (the king's English) plus an indeterminate number of dialects. To a limited extent this is exactly what is happening when people approve or query my account. Thus writing helps to change not only orthodoxy but the notion of orthodoxy and, I believe, of truth and identity, or rather the perception of truth and identity. Quite apart from the fact that writing tends to promote and apply new developments of proof, logic, relevance, or inference (that is, the formalized truth procedures of philosophy, law, and the sciences, for which the existence of writing is a prerequisite at the level of culture), verbal forms reduced to the written take on not only a visual aspect but a stationary character that enables people readily to distinguish differences and to assert similarities—or rather, to do so with new levels of accuracy because of the use of an additional instrument of measuring those differences and similarities by comparing linguistic statements visually as well as orally.

There is a fourth aspect, to which I have already referred, that deeply affects the way in which we represent cultural phenomena in any account but particularly when members of written cultures (of *écricultures*) are attempting to create a ritual text. When we give an account of a ceremony, in writing or in speech, we have to frame it largely in words; there is inevitably a change in channel since we cannot fully represent action, only describe it. (This is not the case with myth and for other types of discourse, informal and formal.) Illustrations would do, of course, but best of all would be a film or video. In presenting an account of a LoDagaa funeral, we can directly represent discourse, even informal discourse, but not the major component of nonverbal action. The formal verbal elements—greetings, songs, speeches—are important but certainly inadequate as an account of or handbook for the ceremony, much more inadequate than a record of the formal myth of the Bagre for a performance of that part of the ceremony; as we have seen in the extract from the Bagre, even the instructions for action, such as those that would constitute a text for a ritual, generally take the form of informal discourse.

So while the words of a ritual can be directly represented (transcribed), the nonverbal acts can be only partially and indirectly represented; collective deeds can only be scripted. A verbal account of nonverbal action means changing the communicative channel. The resulting record may be longer or shorter, more or less selective, depending upon a wide range of factors. In this context one use of the concept of "ritual" comes to refer to formal action less words, while "myth" then tends to cover a certain type of formal spoken act. If the words alone have been written down (myth), then in the future we may have the problem of linking them once again with the (nonrecorded) action, that is, with the ritual; this initial separation in recording constitutes the problematic of the myth-and-ritual school in interpreting the religions of the ancient Near East (Hooke 1933; Goody 1961). Even where ritual has been incorporated in words presented as a text, this record never constitutes a precise handbook, an exact guide to action, since it is necessarily selective—as any account has to be. Much has to be left out (and not simply the intentions and beliefs of the actors), omissions that create a problem for those interpreting ritual texts of a historical kind. While any account is selective, a written account is permanently and more influentially so, the selection providing a model for the future as well as consigning to oblivion all that has been omitted.

Having sketched out what happens when anthropologists or others record a ceremony, we may extrapolate to the situation of a historical or existing written culture with its ritual texts. The extent and use of these vary greatly, but it is worthwhile to suggest some very general distinguishing features on the basis of our knowledge of transformations of contemporary oral cultures, since we cannot acquire any but minimal information about the prewriting phases of historical cultures and hence cannot compare those cultures with their oral predecessors.

From the standpoint of LoDagaa performances, what impresses one about Taoist, Buddhist, or Hindu ceremonies (and the same is true of the Christian Mass) is the tidiness of the proceedings. Formality is stressed to the exclusion of much else. If we regard the form of the Taoist ceremonies of contemporary Taiwan as following the written versions of earlier oral rituals, then the informality of the oral performance has probably been eliminated; if the ceremony was initially composed in writing, then informality was excluded by the way in which the text was constructed. Another way of putting the same point was suggested by the Sinologist K. Schipper when he described even the contemporary rituals of Taiwan as "bureaucratic"; bureaucracies are based on the bureau, the office, the chamber used for written tasks.

One aspect of these characterizations of the written ritual as formal and bureaucratic is that while the ceremony is complex, that complexity is highly repetitive, of the kind that would go well in a written handbook: "Here the priest circles the altar nine times." Similar repetition occurs in the performances of the LoDagaa, actions often being performed three times for a man and four times for a woman. But in written ritual there is not the same rich multiplicity of action one finds in funerals or in the Bagre; the performance is in some ways thinner. There is a significant sense in which the words themselves may also be not exactly meaningless but semantically slim, if only because by being part of a text, they persist over time or space and thus may lose much of their earlier semantic significance. Sanskritic mantras recited in contemporary Taiwan or Japan acquire some new but leaner meanings since they are no longer understood linguistically by the vast majority of those who repeat them. They are less multivocal because more multipurpose.

Informality disappears, and one kind of complexity, too. No conceivable handbook could record the complexity of action in a LoDagaa funeral. Contrast the burial service in the Anglican Book of Common Prayer. That ceremony is a slight affair; it allows little by way of variation for different social persons, just a shift from *him* to *her,* and for burial on land or at sea. That, of course, is what even an oral account of action tends to do. But a written account continues to offer a model of a more compelling kind. As a consequence, orthodoxy (over space and over time) increases; it has to be this service or none at all. Is that perhaps why in rituals such as funerals or weddings unwritten customary action tends to accrete around the written skeleton, putting flesh on the bare bones, just as in medieval England a written dramatic tradition was stimulated by the growth of tropes and embellishments at festival times out of the more rigid framework of the liturgy (Chambers 1903; Axton 1974)?

In written cultures ritual action tends to get extended not so much by variation as by repetition. This feature is remarked upon by Fuller in his analysis of the great temple complex of Madurai in South India.

> The repetitiousness of worship in a Hindu temple is one of its most striking features. Eight times a day, day in and day out, Minaksi and Sundaresvara have to be worshipped. In smaller temples there are usually fewer periods of worship per day, but the theme of constant repetition is nonetheless ubiquitous. (Fuller 1984: 15)

This daily worship is performed so that deities will be pleased and use their power to preserve humanity; it is carried out either in a ritualistic way (according to the doctrine of the Āgamas, the texts were supposedly dictated by Siva himself) or else in a devotionalist manner, after the *bhakti* cults that first emerged in opposition to the more formalistic procedures embodied in the text. Although Fuller emphasizes the general contrast with the order and constraint of a Christian service (1984: 5), there are similar differences of performance within the range of Christian sects, and at the ritualistic end of the continuum both are largely following an order of service laid down in a text. As elsewhere, ritualistic performances are associated with the text, devotion with utterance. A general factor is the commitment of one element to a performance text, a ritual handbook, which necessarily plays down the importance of invention, emphasizes orthodoxy, and enhances the role of the tutor/performer/priest, separating this from the role of the creator/author/prophet.

One other way of putting it is that the orchestration of the written service is rehearsed. There is a virtual absence of the discussions that are so frequently found in the Bagre (as well as in the funerals) of what should come next, a searching around for clues, since in a written service what comes next is literally pre-scribed. Neither the Bagre nor the funeral is rehearsed; to rehearse would be to perform. While it is always necessary for a ritual to be seen to be correct in order to be effective, standards of correctness get tighter with the new means of making such an assessment, and the written text effectively creates a different notion or measure of exactitude. In one way the very formality of the ritual tends to give rise to its opposite; the rehearsed communication between men and gods creates a presentational gap that is filled by the inspired performer, or he who sets aside ritual action in favor of direct communication, leading in some cases to a closer attention to the written word of God (as in the Protestant case) rather than to ritual action, to the myth and the dogma rather than to the rite. What Protestantism did, especially in its radical varieties, was to do away with much existing ritual and concentrate not simply upon the Book but upon its non-ritual aspects. The rituals of the Old Testament, for example, are set aside for allegorical interpretation. So too were many Catholic rituals, including, in some forms of Protestantism, even the commemoration of Christ's birth, which was viewed as a pagan hangover from Roman times. These reformers deconstructed the ritual texts in favor of evangelization, direct communion not only with God but also with God's word, thus going some way toward eliminating the priest.

The intervention of the priest is not intrinsically connected with the use of a ritual text, but if the service is a written one and if writing is not necessarily a priestly monopoly but at least restricted in its practice, and if the word requires interpretation because of its mysterious qualities, then a specialist is likely to become the mediator of God's written word, at least until literacy becomes widespread. So too if the text is written in a different or archaic language. The success of Protestantism in sixteenth-century Europe was intimately connected with the use of the vernacular and with the advent of printing, which replaced the scarce manuscript by mechanically produced books, making them cheaper, more available, and more readable. Hence the priestly role became in principle less important as the mediator, the communicator, of the text.

The relative lack of contextualization of religious action—that is, of rituals that are both priestly and literate—has to do in part with the spread of written religions over many cultures and over the long duration, so that they are less closely tied to any single culture in space or in time. In addition, there is the notion that perpetual service has to be offered to god or temple, for example, in the daily rites in a Christian monastery or in a Hindu temple (Fuller 1984; Prain 1984). Regular services of this kind are not tied to specific occasions such as marriages or first fruits and therefore have a general goal rather than a specific one. The service is fixed, or relatively so, and is used for a wide range of different occasions. We are familiar with the existence of idioms that can be shifted from one ceremony to another—the use of funeral idioms in killing off the old and then creating new statuses is a case in point (E. Goody 1972). But with the ritual text, whole services either need to be multipurpose or else have to concentrate upon the permanent attributes of the godhead rather than the evanescent requests of humanity.

This characteristic represents another side of the formalizing, enduring nature of the written text and the repetitive nature of the rituals it embodies. Performance is linked to the involvement of full-time priests who are no longer family officiants (except in the case of some upper-class households) but mediate more impersonally between the gods and a wider congregation of humans. And this larger clientele provides support through direct payments for services rendered (as mainly in contemporary India) or through long-term endowments (as formerly in Europe). In either case the offering of the daily *puja,* the recurring performance of Masses for the dead, or the repetition of the Ave Maria (neatly linked with a numerical calculation of fewer days in Purgatory in an attempt at supernatural bookkeeping [LeGoff 1984]) seems more characteristic of the rituals (or ritualism) of written cultures than of the rites of oral ones.

4

The Time of Telling and the Telling of Time in Written and Oral Cultures

I n the past my own writing about time—its concepts, its measurement, its organization—has been deliberately quotidian. That is to say, I have tried to look critically at the great cultural generalizations—time in circles, time in straight lines, time autonomous, time embedded—or, rather, to look both critically and sideways at them from a more determinative point of view, asking what particular features of social organization, technology, or other aspects of cultural action would tend to influence concepts of time in certain directions. This I did because it seemed to me too easy, too facile, perhaps too literary to try to characterize chronotypes in largely personal terms, throwing words into the air like confetti and expecting the colored fragments to fall into some enduring pattern. So an encyclopedia article I wrote on the social organization of time looked at the relation of concepts of time to methods of measurement, assessment, in the broadest sense, as well as to modes of production, modes of communication, and religious ideas about the world (1968a). What caught my attention was the insistent emphasis on time in narrative, for narrative has a very special relationship to time, being located at a specific conjunction in time and space, and unwinding in the framework of time.

The Time of Telling: The Written

In the literature of the "high" cultures we know, narrative plays an enormous role. The novel, the film, the play, the opera—nearly all examples of these have a basically narrative structure in which time is of the essence. So too outside the literary sphere; most of the material in newspapers is constructed in the same way, with the telling of news (the day's news) as a systematic account of what happened, where references to time are omnipresent.

In his account of the rise of the novel in the eighteenth century, Ian Watt saw the development of this genre as connected with the radical changes in English society that promoted the growth of realism, individuality, and a new concern with time. No longer relying on traditional narratives, new plots were created that had to be "acted out by particular people in particular circumstances" rather than by "general human types" set in "timeless stories." The genre developed two features of special importance, characterization and the presentation of background. Both were intimately concerned with the particularities not only of names but of time and place. "The characters of a novel," writes Watt, "can only be individualised if they are set in a background of particularised time and place" (1957: 21). Following Locke in *An Essay Concerning Human Understanding,* personal identity is seen as an identity of consciousness through duration in time.

Watt had in mind first and foremost that prototypical English narrative of the period, Defoe's *Robinson Crusoe,* where it is not simply a question of time as sequence or duration, the kind of time found in earlier narratives, but of a precise measurement of the dimensions, the establishment of the time and place of events that provides an illusory realism, a mendacious veracity, that almost takes the novel outside the realm of fiction altogether, making it not simply the story of X, but the history of X. In *Robinson Crusoe* the relationship between the telling of the tale and the telling of time exists both for the writer and for his creature. "The editor," writes Defoe in that deceptively casual way, "believes the thing to be a just history of fact; neither is there any appearance of fiction in it" (Defoe 1927: vii). History demands dates. "I was born in the year 1632, in the city of York, of a good family, tho' not of that county" (Defoe 1927: 1).

Marooned on a desert island, Crusoe became deeply concerned with time, and to control its passage, or his understanding of its passage, he needed pencil and paper. At first his only companions were a dog and two cats, but they served him well, especially the dog. "I wanted nothing that he could fetch me, nor any company that he could make up to me, I only wanted to have him talk to me, but that would not do: as I observed before, I found pen, ink and paper, and I husbanded them to the utmost, and I shall shew, that while my ink lasted, I kept things very exact, but after that was gone I could not" (Defoe 1927: 73).

Keeping things very exact meant above all telling the time.

> After I had been there about ten or twelve days, it came into my thoughts that I should lose my reckoning of time for want of books and pen and ink, and should even forget the Sabbath days from the working days; but to prevent this I cut it with my knife upon a large post, in capital letters, and making it into a great cross I set it up on the shore where I first landed, viz. *I come onshore here on the 30th of Sept. 1659.* Upon the sides of this square post I cut every day a notch with my knife, and every seventh notch was as long again as the rest, and every first day of the month was as long again as that long one, and thus I kept my kalender, or weekly, monthly, and yearly reckoning of time. (Defoe 1927: 72)

That is to say, individual, personal, private markings have to operate within a social, public system for the graphic representation of time, by means of a calendar, which is at once a secular aid and a ritual, liturgical program. The measurement, reckoning, and even conception of time in graphic terms involve giving that dimension a visual and spatial counterpart. Oral discourse takes place in time, written discourse in space and time; the latter is seen, the former unseen.

Keeping things very exact also involved another fascinating use not of graphics but of writing itself, namely, laying out in a list the good and evil aspects of his present situation—exactly like debts and credits, as he remarks—in order better to understand the situation so that he could apply himself to "accommodate" his way of living. But that theme would take us too far from the notion of time as elaborated here, so it is assigned to the postscript.

Defoe's concern with time was by no means unique. The timing of events dominates Laurence Sterne's *Tristram Shandy* (1760) in a more personal but equally exact manner, beginning as it does with the unfortunate incident of his mother interrupting his father at the moment of their monthly coitus: "'Pray, my Dear,' quoth my mother, 'have you not forgot to wind up the clock.'" His father was "one of the most regular men in everything he did," so his son could declare with certainty, "I was begot in the night, betwixt the first Sunday and the first Monday in the month of March, in the year of our Lord one thousand seven hundred and eighteen" (Sterne 1965: 4, 6).

The second chapter of Henry Fielding's *Tom Jones* (1749) opens with more of a spatial placing: "In that part of the western division of this kingdom which is commonly called Somersetshire, there lately lived and perhaps lives still, a gentleman whose name was Allworthy" (Fielding 1950: 3). His *Jonathan Wild* (1743) began (again in the second chapter) on a genealogical rather than chronological note: "It is the custom of all biographers, at their entrance into their work, to step a little backward . . . and to trace up their hero, as the ancients did the Nile, till an incapacity of preceding higher puts an end to their search" (Fielding 1808: 5).

The fine exactitude of timekeeping of course paralleled the meticulousness of bookkeeping. It was scarcely available to writers or desired by their readers until the grandfather clock of Shandy's father and more public varieties in the town hall became part of everyday consciousness, controlled by that tick-tock mechanism, the verge and foliot, the vertical escapement, minimal but immensely important, that was the achievement of the West and one of their few early technical exports to the East (apart from the universally acceptable firearms with which they have long continued to dominate the world). The verge-and-foliot mechanism that gave birth to the modern clock was not, of course, the first method of establishing, that is, measuring, hours (minutes, seconds); so too did the water clock and the candle. But it initiated the domestication, the personalization, of this system, leading to the wristwatch, that quasi-universal aspect of dress in the modern world. And this particularization of time occurred in both everyday and literary contexts.

The Time of Telling: The Spoken

Beyond the realm of print, the recounting of events is often seen as a characteristic form of oral intercourse, just as the storyteller himself is seen as the prototypical creator of narrative tales. Yet here, in my own experience, the problem of evidence raises its shaggy head. Both in written cultures and in oral ones, narrative accounts of events—that is, not simply sequential accounts (emphasizing order) but relational accounts in a stronger sense—are less common and less elaborate in verbal interaction than is often supposed.[1] Visitors arrive and cannot be stopped from telling what happened on the journey; others give accounts of their experience at different moments of their lives. But if these are frequent or prolonged, the tellers run the danger of being described as bores or, worse, old bores. The phrase "As I remember . . ." is the one most likely, at least in literate cultures, to enlarge the generation gap, to raise the level of age discrimination, and to send a shudder down the back of those whose youth in and of itself prohibits the luxury of such reminiscences.

An account requires the suspension not of disbelief but of discourse, at least in the sense of intercourse. The narrative seeks to impose itself on conversation in a hegemonic way, but the nature of interaction is such that we rarely get the chance to finish our account. We return from our European holiday with the story incompletely told, with our slides unshown, partly because the telling and showing demand not so much an attention others are unwilling to give as an inaction they are unwilling to undergo, a suppression of the dialogue/duologue that we accept only in a formal setting, in the ritual or dramatic performance, in the sermon or the lecture, or perhaps in the face of superior authority, to whom we have anyhow little to say—a professor who invites the student to tea, or a queen, premier, or president who asks us to an audience, that is, asks us to provide an audience. In other circumstances all we as tellers are allowed to get away with is the short, pithy narrative of the joke, the end of which is marked by its punch line, which depends upon timing and for which we as hearers are obliged to wait, to pause in our own contribution to the conversation. That is even more the case with print. We remain silent before the written word. Although we can physically discard the novel if the narrator is a bore, he has his day; we remain mute while "real" (or primary) time stands still so that narrative time can take over—or better, since everything we experience is real, so that activity within the tale temporarily excludes everything without.

I do not think this is very different among the LoDagaa of northern Ghana, whom I take as my touchstone of an oral culture, a society without writing, as distinct from the oral tradition within a literate one. Of course, there as everywhere, one has to suffer bores if they hold dominant positions, but in general it is interaction rather than mono-logue that makes for valued intercourse, and long narrative accounts of events belong to the category of monologue. Of course, there are situations where such accounts are called for. In dispute cases, one tries to begin at the beginning and continue to the present, or vice versa. Recounting the sequence of events is inevitably involved in making a case, since one cannot set it out beforehand in writing and take it as read, and since the chronological order is the most logical, the one that communicates the situation most efficiently to the mediator, arbitrator, or judge, or even to the anthropologist as casual spectator.

How about the literary mode in oral cultures, or rather the realm of what I shall refer to by the ugly periphrasis "standardized oral forms"? Here our attachment to a literary background may mislead. We are accustomed to thinking of standardized oral forms in terms of folk-tale, legend, epic, and myth, that is, in narrative terms, together of course with song, in which music, voice, and possibly dance are inextricably involved—in my experience, the lyric does not exist as words alone (see Bowra 1962; Finnegan 1970). All these forms are widely reported, and yet I want to argue that they are not always widely used.

Let me take first of all the most obvious question, that of folktales. These display a very definite narrative structure, although their char-acters are a mixture of people, animals, and gods (often God, in fact). While they are rarely specific as to absolute time, "once upon a time" being more likely a beginning for these tales than the type of opening found in *Tristram Shandy* or *Robinson Crusoe*, they do offer the lis-tener a sequence of tightly interconnected events to follow. They are short and limited in number, and the stories are largely for children. It is customary for those brought up on nineteenth-century views of popular literature, fostered by German and European nationalisms, to regard such tales as the *disjecta membra* of earlier oral cultures, as the survivals of myths of greater significance. In fact, that is not at all the case, or rarely is. We find strikingly similar short tales distributed throughout the oral cultures of Africa, where they have not only a remarkably similar form and content but also a similar role. Here I speak from my own experience and am unsure how far this knowledge can be generalized. While this experience does not at all agree with the statements of other writers, when you examine these accounts in detail it is clear that the context of telling has often been recalled from their youth or from the recollections of other people, and the stories have been recorded in specially constructed situations. But, with one exception, I have never seen adults gather round of an evening telling such tales to one another. When I heard them told in natural settings, it has always been adults to children (into which category the visiting anthropologist easily fits), or more likely children to one another. Adults occasionally refer to such tales, but by and large in much the same way as we would refer to Little Red Riding Hood or Jack and the Beanstalk. As for those who take the content of such tales as a sample of the thought of oral cultures, it is no wonder that they end up with notions of their "primitive" nature; an African scholar viewing Snow White in the same way would come to similar conclusions about European cultures. Any literary form is only part, at times important, at times less significant, of the complexity of human thought and action that we call culture.

Let me turn to the more extended forms, legend, epic, and myth, and ask how characteristic they are of oral cultures. It is perhaps not worth spending much time on the first of these concepts as a category of oral discourse, since the word itself is derived from the medieval Latin of the twelfth century and refers to that "meet to be read," that is, to stories of saints' lives intended to be read at matins *(la légende dorée),* or later, in the sixteenth century, "a popular traditional tale, more or less fabulous," legends centering around real persons but embroidered by the imagination, as in the legend of Roland or Faust. The equivalent in the oral cultures of Africa would be the clan histories I discuss later.[2]

The legend of Roland is known not only as a "song" *(chanson)* but as an epic, a narrative usually in verse. The word *epic* is derived from the Greek *epos* and used specifically to refer to the classical works such as the *Iliad, Odyssey,* or *Aeneid,* whereas the more mysteriously resonant term *myth* is often applied—by Kirk (1970), for example—to the

Mesopotamian Gilgamesh. All these early forms were strongly narrative, firmly grounded in space and time—not to the extent of most films or novels produced for "*le grand public*," perhaps not to the degree demanded by the Aristotelian unities, but using time and space as central aspects of the organizational framework.

Following the research of Parry and Lord, the Homeric epics at least (it is not, of course, the same for Virgil nor later for Milton) were held to be oral compositions, of the same general kind as the Yugoslav epics the Harvard classicists recorded in so pioneering a fashion, taking their place next to such classic productions of the so-called oral mode as Gilgamesh and the Rig Veda, though the latter is hardly narrative. In Chadwick's theory they were characteristic features of the Heroic Age, the age of warrior courts that encouraged the production of long narratives telling of fabulous struggles (Chadwick 1912).

The problem is not so much locating these narratives in their socio-historical context as seeing them as typical productions of oral cultures. First, the discussion is often based on a failure to distinguish between the products of oral intercourse, of a so-called oral tradition, in societies with writing (such as Yugoslavia) and those of oral cultures (those without writing at all). In societies with writing there is consequently a tendency to treat the two traditions as distinct rather than interacting. Second, when we look at the societies where the classical epics flourished, these were all ones with writing. Third, in the area that has been the largest source of compositions from oral cultures, Africa, there is remarkably little legend or epic, a fact noted by Ruth Finnegan in her comprehensive review of "oral literature" in that continent (1970). We find some epics in the warrior groups of the Saharan fringe, recorded by Christiane Ségou, Amhaté Ba, Claude Meillassoux, and others, but these works are obviously influenced by the traditions of written Muslim culture coming from the Mediterranean. They are largely the products of professional singers (griots), who adapt their versions to the particular audience whose forebears they honor.

How does myth fit into this perspective from the standpoint of narrative and of oral cultures? I use the term *myth* in a simplistically concrete way, not to refer, as many do, to the cosmology (or mythology) of simple societies, reconstructed from fragmentary references in prayers, folktales, recitations, and commentaries, but to speak of a genre, a standard oral form, of long oral recitations, not fabulous in the legendary sense (though already in Greek one meaning of the word refers to the mistaken or outworn beliefs of others), but concerned with supernatural as well as human beings. Myth as cosmology does not exist as a specific discourse, the equivalent of the literary text, except, of course, in the writings of the observer; myth as a recitation, on the other hand, is a primary construction of the actors themselves, taking a standardized oral form. Contrary to expectation, such lengthy recitations are not common features of oral cultures. We do occasionally find them, and it is a recitation that I have recorded many times to which I refer briefly in the next paragraphs. But their distribution is very intermittent, found in one community but not in the next, and insofar as they are characteristic of any general type in Africa, it is the nonheroic rather than the heroic type of society—the "tribe," not the state.

The Bagre myth of the LoDagaa I have already described. In the context of the uses and types of time, what struck me about the myth was the relative lack of importance placed upon narrative, and hence upon narrative time or narrative space. That is to say, there was a plot in the shape of a plan, but not in the specific sense of structured narrative.[3] Part of the reason emerges when we think back to the myth-and-ritual school that flourished in classical and Near Eastern studies earlier this century and that received at least part of its inspiration from Jane Harrison's 1914 work *Ancient Art and Ritual,* and which in turn owed much to the Frazerian influence on classics in the works of Cornford, Cooke, and others (and these owed something to the contributions of the Durkheimian school). Just as W. Robertson Smith had maintained there was no belief without its ritual (1889), so too Hooke and others made the same claim about myth and ritual: that the one was the verbal counterpart of the other. As a general theory of myth, the claim is inadequate, but it works in particular cases. The White Bagre is one of these.

While the Bagre as a whole is recited during the ceremonies, the White Bagre is an account of the rituals the neophytes are actually undergoing. These ceremonies proceed over a period of some months, and on each occasion when one takes place, the myth is recited up to the point that has been reached in the performances. But although it is an account of the ritual, it is certainly not exhaustive; rather, it is a post hoc recapitulation from which much is omitted but certain salient features recalled, as if to emphasize the importance of these for both the neophytes and the initiated alike. Sequential time is involved in the account of the ceremonies; one follows the other in a set order that is linked to the seasons, partly for the sake of the provisions needed for food and beer, but also to stress the value of crops (and of the performance itself) by first imposing, then gradually lifting, a series of food and other taboos. But duration too is stressed by the many references to the time spent in the various activities, and by the repeated injunction to go around calling all the participants to come together in two days' time.

To a few phases of the ceremony are attached short narrative incidents resembling folktales, their attractiveness serving as much as anything to fix that phase in the mind of Speaker and listener. At the same time the loose framework of an explanation is provided, though once again there is little that people did not already know. The very beginning takes the form of setting the stage at an undetermined time and place in the past when troubles were heaped upon the head of one man and his family, presumed to be an ancestor. As a result, he went to a diviner and was told he had to perform the Bagre so that these problems would cease to worry him. What follows is an account of what he did in the past and what we now are doing in the present, an account and a performance that themselves amount to the conquest of time and space. The ceremony resembles a Mass, only it is perhaps less like a deliberate reenactment, for what happened then is happening right now. There is no progression between past and present. This is no miracle play representing the death of Hussein, no seder commemorating the exodus from Egypt; it is the thing itself, with the same significance as the original act. The same events occur. In one ceremony God comes down to earth; he did so then and does so now. In another the ancestors return to their old hearth and drink the beer that is being brewed for the participants. It is the fact that these ceremonies involve replication that makes the ancestors so important because, in the absence of a Book of Hours or a Book of Common Prayer, the structure of legitimation rests on the memory of old men (prompting each other) as to what their predecessors did. The ancestors are the experienced old men who have passed on, leaving their successors to cope inadequately but as best they can (that is how the LoDagaa put it to themselves). Like God (and gods), ancestors too are both there and here, both were and are, conquering not only time but space as well.

The conquest of time does not necessarily mean the abandonment of narrative. In the prophetic religions, which are the Religions of the Book, the major yearly ceremonies are recapitulations of the life of the Master, a life cycle rehearsed as an annual cycle (even a weekly cycle in the case of the Mass). Nevertheless, the narrative structure of the White Bagre, as recited in Birifu, is extremely weak. That is not always the case elsewhere. A version recorded by my collaborator, Kum Gandah, in the neighboring settlement of Lawra in 1977, which we have transcribed and translated, includes a long prose account of the legend of how the clan migrated and came to settle where it now is (Gandah and Goody 1995). In other words, it describes the path of the ancestors *(saakum sor)*, which is both the actual path they took (and to which sacrifices are always made in the course of the Bagre) and the path (the ways) they followed then and which we still follow now. Much of the imagery of the Bagre has to do with a quest, with mankind being led along, then off, the right path, usually by the beings of the wild, who are both revealers of culture and tricksters at the same time. Here time in the sense of sequence (narrative) is important but time in the sense of unilinearity is not, for the journey of the ancestors results in their meeting new neighbors who teach them to perform the Bagre, a ritual they knew in the past but had since abandoned and forgotten. So in this case, too, the recitation about the past merges into, conforms with, present action.

This Lawra example is the only example I know of an extended clan legend of this kind among the LoDagaa, and it seems to have been elaborated specifically in the context of the Bagre—in the context, that is, of the recitation. In every village you visit, lineage elders can give some account of the migration of the clan, and often enough one finds the story confirmed by inhabitants at the other villages mentioned. But these are at best fragmentary, at worst shreds and patches, hardly narratives in any meaningful sense.

To the south of the noncentralized, tribal LoDagaa lies the ancient kingdom of Gonja, which has been influenced by Islam and by written Arabic in a very marginal way.[4] In this kingdom narrative "histories," legends, of events abound, especially around the person of the conquering hero, Jakpa, the Lord of the Towns, the founder of the kingdom. These accounts are highly segmentary, with very different versions being given in different divisions of the kingdom, by different memorialists and by different ethnic groups within the state. The nearest approach to a national legend of the ruling group is the drum recital of the Kuntungkure drummers of Damongo, the present capital. But this is not narrative in any significant sense. It consists of the drum titles of a series of chiefs or chiefships, the two being again confounded since praise to one's ancestors is praise to the present incumbent and vice versa. These titles are recited in archaic or "deep" Gonja, and even the words, let alone the wider reference to events, are intelligible to only a few. Indeed, one might say that their present authority in solving disputes, when the drummer is called to play and interpret, depends upon just this, because they can be turned to support almost any cause, like the ambiguous pronouncements of other oracles, more distant in time, or the forecasting of events that are seized upon in newspaper astrology.

In addition, there exists an eighteenth-century chronicle in Arabic covering a period of some fifty years with annual comments on the significant events, some dated in calendrical fashion, and beginning with a version of an earlier legend of the conquest. Various copies are in the possession of the priestly Muslims of certain divisions, where they are kept as a legitimizing treasure (Wilks et al. 1987). The written chronicle provides a stark contrast with the oral forms, clearly bringing out the potential consequences for "history" of even a very restricted use of writing. Nevertheless, in Gonja both are treated in much the same fashion. Since very few can understand Arabic and no one recalls the events that the chronicle recounts, we are dealing with much the same situation for the actors as with the drum titles. But for the future historian the potential consequences are very different.

The legends told in the various localities differ in character from the written chronicle (as well as from the drum history), being less structured in form and largely narrative in content, telling mainly of what happened when the Lord of the Towns first came to those parts and how he was received locally. In these oral histories little or nothing is found of later events, apart from accounts of some recent happenings in the latter half of the nineteenth century. Otherwise virtually all is concentrated on what was the beginning of things for the Gonja and for their commoners as they arrived in the country, that is, how they got there and where they came from. Once again the past is not altogether divorced from the present, and while we certainly cannot explain everything in these legends by reference to the contemporary state of affairs, in many cases one element is that of a charter for current claims of the kind Malinowski posited. There are some fairly gross examples of such manipulation of narrative at the time when it was necessary to make claims about rank and territory to the colonial conquerors (Goody 1954), and today, too, one rarely hears of matters that do not support the status quo, unless the complaint comes from some subordinate group, a slighted dynasty, or an unsuccessful prince.

Given the pressures of local interests, it is not surprising that the versions vary. But in fact they vary very much more and in different ways than this factor alone would suggest, telling different and incompatible stories about the conquering hero and those associated with him. It would be impossible for any Gonja to attempt to reconcile them, or even a sample, within the bounds of oral culture, partly because of the ambiguities about time (chronological time) and space. Even when writing makes it possible to set one version beside another and to try to interdigitate events, resolve contradictions, and distinguish the personae, there is little possibility of linking them into a consecutive, time-oriented document. The late paramount chief Yagbumwura Timu II, previously the minister J. A. Braimah, set about this task in a series of largely unpublished manuscripts, putting forward his interpretation of a number of these sources in a coherent but impressionistic fashion (Braimah n.d.). Even more-rigorous literary scholarship would serve only to document variability and bring to light contradictions; it would not produce a synthetic account. It is true that some early literates within Gonja society might have taken the various Jakpa stories and strung them together into a rather picaresque legend. Indeed, this seems to have been the way that a number of longer versions of epics or legends were constructed during the Heroic Age, that is, during the infancy of written literatures. But here no synthesis occurred. Like the state itself, historical narrative was highly decentralized; the "overkingdom," as I have called it on the medieval Irish model, had no national history, apart from the Gonja chronicle and the drum titles.

The Gonja, then, are greater employers of narrative forms than the LoDagaa. While they have a similar repertoire of folktales, not only is legend more developed but so too is the use of narrative accounts in disputes that come to court—the LoDagaa were more likely to have recourse to the bow and arrow, and even now have not developed a court oratory of the kind their neighbors have. On the other hand, the Gonja have nothing like the Bagre.

I have so far been referring to the White Bagre of the LoDagaa, which we might see as the equivalent of a (written) ritual text, except that it does not act as a guidebook that serves to prompt, indeed to dominate, such performances, as in the case of Religions of the Book. The Black Bagre does show a greater narrative content, even if chronological time itself (and even sequential time in a storytelling sense) plays only a minimal part, for the second part of the recitation expands on the notion of a quest, a seeking after truth, which in a much more simplified form constitutes the framework of the White Bagre. One of the two (first) men, described as companions rather than as brothers, sets out on a journey, during the course of which he learns, partly from God, mainly from the beings of the wild, about culture, how to perform those things essential to human life as the LoDagaa presently experience it; from God how to procreate, from the beings of the wild how to smelt iron, grow crops, make weapons, brew beer. The narrative accounts of how these processes are carried out are essentially based on contemporary ways of doing things, except that the local production of iron disappeared soon after the beginning of the century with the advent of mass-produced European goods but remains a major part of the recitation, an increasingly archaic feature.

If the narrative element in this part of the myth is stronger than in the first, it turns around these technical processes, although not exclusively so. The younger man's quest after knowledge also brings him face-to-face with spiritual forces: with God in the Above, with the beings of the wild here on earth, and at one point with the Earth shrine, or rather the skin (surface) of the earth *(tenggaan)*, and this involves a discussion of philosophical issues about, for example, the problem of good and evil, of why we should follow certain prohibitions (taboos) and carry out certain actions (sacrifices). So while a narrative framework exists, both for the Black Bagre itself and for the constituent incidents (for instance, the making of iron), these are not tightly structured from the standpoint of time. In the first place, here too we are talking about the past and the present at the same moment. What happened then is happening now; in any case, the "then" is the vaguely defined time of Genesis rather than the more precise time of the Gonja chronicles. In the second place, much of the meat of the Black Bagre, in its more elaborate versions, has to do with speculations that are foreign to the narrative mode and which bypass considerations of space and time since their significance is seen as universal. It is not so much that the LoDagaa are concerned with an original Dreamtime, as has been said of the Australian Aborigines. "Once upon a time" would (if it were possible to translate it) sound as childish to them as it does to us. Rather, in ritual and myth then and now are one and the same, or at least merged into a timeless unity.

Given this general situation, we need to ask the question of why it is that the myths of oral societies presented to us by many scholars place such a heavy emphasis on narrative, on story, on sequence. I think here specifically of the myths, or snippets of narrative, used in works such as Lévi-Strauss's magisterial volumes on South America, *Mythologiques* (1964–71). There are no doubt some broad regional differences in oral style, form, and content between Africa and America; animals do not normally play a central part in African myths as distinct from folktales, since in the graver forms of discourse the actors are humans and their gods. But I suggest that the widespread predominance of narrative is largely a matter of the demands and expectations of the European observer, although a matter partly of the context of myth and partly of the reduction of oral forms to written ones.

The demands of a European observer, coming into the society from beyond, are often precisely for a story, a narrative. Even if it were possible to recite the Bagre outside the ceremonial situation, it would be impossible to tell the story of the first part, and not easy for the second. Any kind of summary would be difficult, although one could easily reproduce one of the stories or folktales that, like nodules of flint in chalk, are embedded in the recitation, for example, that of the guinea cock and his mate fighting over food and sex, which marks the beginning of a particular ceremony. What would inevitably be omitted would be the account of ritual or the more philosophical passages, which would be suppressed in favor of the more salient narrative, giving the impression that the story, a fabulous story, is what such recitations are about. Until recently this was the dominant impression about these oral forms because myths were rarely recorded verbatim; most could be recited only in the ritual context, and even if the observer was present and very fluent with the language, it was impossible for him or her to write down a long recitation word for word. Outside the context of performance, the recitation was likely to undergo considerable change. Only recently has the position altered as the result of the introduction of the portable cassette recorder, although in countries with more advanced technologies it has been possible, as in the case of Parry and Lord's research, to make sound recordings over a somewhat longer period.

The Telling of Time: The Oral and Written

There is a final point that has been one of the subliminal themes of this discussion and that has to do with the telling of time rather than the time of telling. One element in the difference between the use of time and narrative has to do not simply with differences between complex and simple cultures, but more specifically with differences in the means of communication. While the measurement of time is not the result of the introduction of writing (much less of alphabetic writing), the shift from "natural" markers to abstract markers represents a development of great importance, to science as to daily life, and this shift influences not only the content but the structure of literary achievement. Although these changes are not directly due to writing per se, they are dependent upon graphic or conceptual lines being drawn (and the drawing of lines is a basic graphic accomplishment), for instance, in terms of an era, whose point of departure has to be recorded and the subsequent dates fixed by a regular written procedure. The concept of an era is not the kind of thing that develops in oral cultures.

Despite, or perhaps because of, the difficulties of measuring chronological time in oral cultures, there is often considerable internal pressure toward the telling of time. When I lived among the LoDagaa I was frequently asked to tell the time from my watch, whereas normally one would refer to the position of the sun; that was a matter not only of the prestige accorded to my chronometer and to the demands of the new schedules imposed by paid labor, but also of a more general desire for increased accuracy. It can be aggravating not to meet people on the right day and at the right hour (the hour, unlike the day itself, is an arbitrary concept). But the desire for greater precision was perhaps more evident in the requests made to me to say how many "moons" would elapse before, say, the first rains, for it was realized that my written calibration of time could bypass the counting of uncountable moon-months (uncountable for technical reasons to do with the intercalation of lunar and solar cycles) and the need to wait for the appearance of a certain insect, even if the latter might possibly give a more accurate prediction, being responsive to environmental factors in a way that an abstracted calendar cannot be.

But it was not only these practical uses of writing-based time measurement that were valued by the nonliterate LoDagaa and their neighbors. In the account books of an interesting Vai figure in Liberia, called Ansumana Sonie, Cole, Scribner, and I found he had written down in Arabic numerals the exact dates of events, especially birth dates, in the manner that was common in European family Bibles (see Goody 1987). There was no particular reason for this recording, especially since the widespread use of the time of birth for astrological purposes in the Chaldean-derived traditions that spanned the Old World from the Blasket Islands to the Philippines was not to be found in this peripheral area of Islam. Sonie used birth and subsequent dates to play with in unexpected ways, for example, to calculate elapsed time between events. Part of his interest in doing so may have derived from the constant preoccupation of the written cultures surrounding him with dates of birth, used to calculate age and to mark the annual transition at birthdays and other anniversaries. Even where not marked in the home environment, these soon became a preoccupation with schoolchildren in the Third World, even where no registration exists. Date of birth, like given name and family name, was soon incorporated as an essential feature of a card of identity. And the birthday party for their children was one of the major festivals adopted by the African urban bourgeoisie in Ghana to bring together school friends and neighbors as distinct from kin. It was a strong but perhaps unintentional marker that distinguished them and us from their brethren who had not been to school.

What I am suggesting here is not simply that the advent of writing makes a difference to time measurement, the recording of events, and people's conceptions of time, a well-established theme, but that oral cultures are often only too prepared to accept these innovations. Even with their system of pictographic protowriting, the Native Americans achieved the recording of annual events in, for example, Lone Dog's Winter Count among the Dakota. If such forms of time recording might well have been influenced by the European invaders of their country, then the important role of the calendar in Central American graphic systems provides more irreproachable evidence of the early tendency of writing systems to develop chronological chronotypes, modes of reckoning time.

Time and Narrative in Oral and Written History

All this bears upon the emergence of history as we know it and its differentiation (at least the differentiation of the narrative history espoused by Lawrence Stone [1979]) from other narrative forms and more generally from wider concerns with the passage of time. Of course, concepts of time as well as the implications of time are always there; people look back at their personal as well as their collective past, in the latter case both genealogically and in an event-linked form *(l'histoire événementielle)*. But the selection of kin and events is certainly more dominated by the present than is the case when the genealogy or the events have been recorded in writing, so that the notion of the past as a charter for the present carries more (though not exclusive) weight. Genealogies cannot themselves, even when written, be regarded as history, since while they embody sequence, they hardly entail consequence. Indeed, somewhat the same can be said of chronicles of the kind found in Gonja, which incorporate measured time, a simple recording, but again not consequence, not narrative. Clan legends, on the other hand, do utilize narrative, often in a relatively tight sense, at least with regard to space. Time is inevitably more difficult to be precise about.

As others have argued, the oral genealogy is often more a statement about space (especially social space) than one about time, since among other things it often represents the contemporary, or near-contemporary, distribution of living groups as much as the relations between dead individuals. Such a use of the past is, of course, also known in written history, but the difference lies, importantly, in the matter of degree and the fact that the written raises in an acute form problems of the intercalation of the past and the present, the written and the oral, the functions and structures of views of the past and their value relative to the present. It is an opposition, a conflict, that was dramatically brought out in the use of Tiv genealogies in twentieth-century colonial West Africa or of the Domesday Book in colonial England under the Norman invaders (Clanchy 1979). In the first case, conflict arose between the colonial administrators and the Tiv over the oral genealogies written down by administrators fifty years earlier and no longer in accord with the local views of the "past" that were so highly conditioned by present concerns. So too with the Domesday Book, where a bookkeeping of conquered England at one instance in time continued to serve as a point of reference for law courts for the next few centuries (Goody and Watt 1963; Goody 1986a: 160).

I do not mean that there can be no accounts of the past of oral cultures, either by observers or by the actors themselves. Both, however, differ from accounts based upon written records, which, following the usage adopted by archaeologists and other scholars when they speak of prehistory, I refer to as history. It is certainly possible to use the word *history* in a more inclusive sense for all accounts of the past (the manifestation of "historicity," to use a neologism, ugly in shape and in implications) and to put the same term in quotes for the more specialist, literate form, as I have elsewhere suggested one might do with logic and "logic." But that solution seems a cumbersome one.

The relative absence of history of and within oral cultures is not at all a matter of their "childlike" nature. It is rather a question of a lack of means. It may also be a question of the lack of interest (the two are closely intertwined), but I am not altogether happy about the latter notion, since as with the pressure from below for greater precision with the measurement of time, so too one of the first "scholarly" activities of newly literate groups in contemporary Africa is to write their own "histories." On one hand, this activity is undoubtedly promoted by contact with other historiographic traditions, those of Islam and Europe. On the other hand, the impulse seems very widespread. And it is not simply a question of people having history in their heads waiting to be written down. The existence of new cognitive tools enables people to undertake new cognitive tasks. To speak about their historicity or sense of history in an unrefined way is to abandon important distinctions; to be able to "read" the stars in an oral culture does not have the same implications as to be able to read a (written) text. To extend concepts metaphorically in such an overly relativistic way is to meet the other not face-to-face but back-to-back; to force our "history," our reading, on them is to abandon history, to see development or evolution (in all their complexities) as stopping with the apes. We are indeed different, but are we so different? What we need is neither oppositions nor identities but effective discriminations that are contextualized by the questions we ask and by the tasks we undertake.

There is a similar but not identical problem with narrative. I am not suggesting that the narrative form is totally alien to oral cultures, only that it is less common than often supposed, and what does exist is more loosely structured than in cultures with writing. It is difficult to measure the tightness or looseness of narrative, but I suggest the following simple criteria may be relevant:

1. The preciseness of the location in time and space (that is, the presentation of background)
2. The development of characterization
3. The proportion of nonnarrative material
4. The integration of the plot, by which I mean the degree of substitutability of segments and the way these lock together

The relative lack of emphasis on narrative is partly a matter of the separation of genres. Myth in the shape of the Bagre is not simply a narrative; it does a great deal more work that for Western audiences would be allocated to other written genres, not simply literary ones in the restricted sense. It is the point I have made about the comparison between the Yugoslav epics, Homeric epics, and oral myth. And it is not simply a question of exclusive genres but of an exclusive conception of the literary and the other, representing not only a radical division between fiction and reality, but also the application of a notion that literature is the equivalent of the literary and neglects other written material of a type that would be part of the more inclusive set of genres that characterize the undifferentiated or less differentiated oral world.

In conclusion, the narrative form itself, storytelling in the prototypical sense, is often seen as characteristic of the oral; yet it is a less common genre than is often thought, becoming more pronounced in cultures undergoing the early stage of the influence of writing.[5] Storytelling requires some measure of hegemonic domination of the kind that an adult can impose upon a child's time, indeed is often asked to do so, but which adults more rarely agree to have imposed upon themselves, unless in a formal ritual or dramatic situation where the story is literally enacted, or when they are alone (or even in company) with a book. Then they are temporarily out of "real" time and into narrative time, and the times, the telling of time and the time of telling (or time told), are out of joint.[6]

Postscript: Crusoe, the Table, and His Mind

Watt has discussed the work of Defoe in the context of the rise of the English novel and the extension of the reading public. Robinson Crusoe was seen as the embodiment of the qualities called for by the mercantile capitalism that expanded so rapidly in England after 1688. But Crusoe reflected not only changes in the modes of production (and these had already occurred even if industrial capitalism had yet to emerge) but shifts in the modes of communication, not simply the consequences of the invention of printing but those of the development of the whole world of writers, printers, publishers, booksellers, and—most important—a wider public that could read and acquire books (or at least Bunyan's *Pilgrim's Progress*).

Crusoe obtained some books from the shipwreck as well as the pen, ink, and paper with which he began to keep a record of time. But he used his literacy skills for yet another purpose, to draw up "the state of my affairs in writing" (Defoe 1927: 74). This he does as a list or table in dualistic fashion, setting Evil on one side and Good on the other, just like "debtor and creditor." Lists and tables of a less semantically complex kind were the currency of many early written civilizations (Goody 1977a). Indeed, they are characteristic literate achievements, comparing synchronically that which speech lets one examine only diachronically. The result was remarkable, for it enabled him to weigh up his condition, externalize it on paper, and then get on with his way of living. The whole passage is worth quoting as a dramatic illustration of the role of writing at a level that is at once both cognitive and practical.

> I now began to consider seriously my condition, and the circumstances I was reduced to, and I drew up the state of my affairs in writing, not so much to leave them to any that were to come after me, for I was likely to have but few heirs, as to deliver my thoughts from daily poring upon them, and afflicting my mind; and as my reason began now to master my despondency, I began to comfort my self as well as I could, and to set the good against the evil, that I might have something to distinguish my case from worse, and I stated it very impartially, like debtor and creditor, the comforts I enjoyed against the miseries I suffered, thus:

I am cast upon a horrible desolate island, void of all hope of recovery.	But I am alive, and not drown'd as all my ship's company was.
I am singl'd out and separated, as it were, from all the world to be miserable.	But I am singl'd out too from all the ship's crew to be spar'd from death; and he that miraculously sav'd me from death, can deliver me from this condition.
I am divided from mankind, a solitaire, one banish'd from humane society.	But I am not starv'd and perishing on a barren place, affording no sustenance.

I have not clothes to cover me.	But I am in a hot climate, where if I had clothes I could hardly wear them.
I am without any defence or means to resist any violence of man or beast.	But I am cast on an island, where I see no beasts to hurt me, as I saw on the coast of Africa; and what if I had been shipwreck'd there?
I have no soul to speak to, or relieve me.	But God wonderfully sent the ship near enough to the shore, that I have gotten out so many necessary things as will either supply my wants, or enable me to supply my self even as long as I live.

Upon the whole here was an undoubted testimony, that there was scarce any condition in the world so miserable, but there was something negative or something positive to be thankful for in it; and let this stand as a direction from the experience of the most miserable of all conditions in this world, that we may always find in it something to comfort our selves from, and to set in the description of good and evil, on the credit side of the account.

Having now brought my mind a little to relish my condition, and given over looking out to sea to see if I could spy a ship, I say, giving over these things, I began to apply my self to accommodate my way of living, and to make things as easy to me as I could. (Defoe 1927: 75–76)

Just as writing enabled Crusoe to conquer (that is, organize) time, so too it enabled him to conquer his difficulties and organize his thoughts.

5
Writing and Revolt in Bahia

The greatest forced migration of peoples in the history of the world followed upon Columbus's discovery of the New World. In 1495, on his second voyage, he brought with him two African slaves from the Iberian peninsula (Rout 1976: 22). Following the drying up of the supply of white slaves from the Near East as the result of the Turkish conquest of Constantinople, there had been an increased flow of slaves into Europe from the western coast of Africa.

Slaves for the New World were first imported from Spain into Hispaniola in 1502 to help produce the newly introduced sugar crop (Mintz 1985). But the main shippers of slaves directly from Africa were the Portuguese, who took them to Cartagena, on the Caribbean shore of Colombia, where they were then sold to the Spanish colonists. They came largely from the Guinea coast of West Africa, the preferred supply for Spain, while those from Angola went mostly to the Portuguese colony of Brazil. The day before embarkation Angolan slaves were usually assembled in a nearby church, sometimes in the main square of the port, in order to be baptized. As far as the ecclesiastical authorities were concerned, it was essential that this sacrament be performed, since the missionizing aspect of the slave trade was often seen, at least by the Church, as the most compelling reason for its existence. "As a prelude to the perfunctory ceremony to follow, the priest walked among the rows of captives, assigning a Christian name to each and handing him a paper with his name written on it lest he forget it" (Bowser 1974:

47). Indeed, according to Henry Koster, the Angolan slaves in Brazil bore the mark of the royal crown on their breasts, which "denotes that they have undergone the ceremony of baptism" (1816: 198).

The renaming of slaves, who were by definition kinless persons, in fact nonpersons, was nothing new. I have known individuals of slave origin in the Gonja town of Salaga in northern Ghana who had been given names such as "I am here," supposedly an answer to the question "Where are you?" Such new names served to cut the individuals off from their kinfolk, their society, and even humanity itself, and at the same time emphasized their servile status. In the case of the Portuguese slaves from Angola, the Catholic Church not merely legitimized but sacralized enslavement by the bestowal of a new name—a Christian name, as we still say in English—that effected an enforced conversion. Free Africans had become Christians and slaves.

However, the renaming was not in itself sufficient; the new name had to be written down and handed to the individual. To the magic of the spoken word was added the hocus-pocus of the written one, which supposedly transformed the religious status of someone whose social life had already been totally overturned by purchase or by the sword. To think about this act is to realize its terrifying authoritarianism. The paper was intended to convey information to the slave's purchaser in the New World. But at the same time it provided a card of identity, which at one level effected the change of identity it purported to record.

There are countless other examples of the use of writing for what can be called magico-religious purposes: the burning of paper money before Chinese altars, the Tibetan Buddhist prayer wheels turning the pages of prayer books, messages stuffed into the Temple walls in Jerusalem, the drinking of the ink in which Qur'anic verses have been written on wooden tablets, the Egyptian letters to gods and to forefathers, and, to bring it nearer home, notes to Santa Claus. All these cases obviously occur when religions are written and, except for the Egyptian and Chinese examples, written in an alphabetic script; they were religions with sacred texts and at the same time religions of conversion. These facts were not accidentally associated.

In this chapter I want to argue for a positive relationship between the presence of writing, the nature of social protest, and particular features of the religious system in the context of the concrete situation of African slaves in the New World. In the early nineteenth century, as today, blacks comprised more than half of the population of the tropical countries of South America with access to the Atlantic seaboard. Originating in Africa, they were brought over as slaves, mainly to work on the sugar estates.[1] The slave trade itself started soon after the beginning of the colonial period and continued until the middle of the nineteenth century, although owing to the frequency of manumission and of "miscegenation" in comparison with North America, at least after 1830, a significant proportion of that population consisted of freed men and women.[2] But if manumission lessened the pressure to escape, it also stimulated the importation of new slaves for the labor force (Sharp 1976: 146–47). So did the prospect of abolition. After the beginning of the British-inspired campaign to end the slave trade, the numbers imported into Brazil increased steadily, from 130,000 a decade in the eighteenth century to 387,000 between 1840 and 1850. Indeed, Brazil was estimated to have a population of 3,817,000 in 1817–18, of which 2,515,000 were *preto* (black) and *pardo* (mulatto); of these, 585,000 were at that time free, and blacks constituted only 15 percent of this number (Kent 1970: 335).

Protests against slavery by slaves themselves often took the form of escape, with the runaways establishing relatively short-lived maroon communities *(palenques* or *quilambos)* in defended villages in inaccessible places—and occasionally longer-lasting ones, as in the well-known case of Palmares, containing over five thousand escaped slaves and enduring nearly seventy years, from 1630 to 1697 (Genovese 1981; Price 1973; Friedemann and Cross 1979; Schwartz 1970: 315; Kent 1970: 337–38). Flight, writes Frederick Bowser in regard to Peru, was the most common form of protest (1974: 330). But revolts of freedmen as well as of slaves also occurred and were facilitated by the fact that even slaves were often allowed to carry arms and were sometimes used to control other slaves.[3] According to Gilberto Freyre, these slave forces were developed in the course of family feuds among the ruling class; in time they defended not only the Great House but the whole country against the Dutch and the entire class against runaway slaves (1946: 358). It is the series of uprisings that took place in the rich sugar-growing province of Bahia, both in the city of São Salvador itself and in the surrounding countryside, between 1807 and 1835 that are the focus of the present discussion.

Of these the revolt of 1835 was the most serious, giving rise to fears of another massacre like the one that had occurred in Saint-Domingue (later Haiti) in 1791, with the "Black Jacobins" under Toussaint-Louverture murdering whites and taking possession of the country. This they might well have done in São Salvador, the capital of Bahia and a center for the importation of slaves until the middle of the nineteenth century, as nonwhites formed seven-eighths of the town's population of 125,000. Although such revolts drew the attention of white Brazilians to the danger of adding to the black population, the need for labor (especially for the coffee plantations after 1835), the reluctance of the dominant class to participate in manual work, and the constant emancipation of slaves (often with the help of black Catholic fraternities and the practice of rotating credit) meant a continual demand for new recruits.[4] Many of these later imports were of Yoruba origin (Nagos, from *Anango*, the term by which they were known in most of South America). Their language became the lingua franca of Bahian Africans from the turn of the century until the 1860s, and it was freedmen and mulattos from this group who, drafted into trade and crafts rather than the plantations, played a leading role in the events of 1835.[5] Yoruba slaves continued to be shipped from Whydah, the main port of Dahomey, long after the suppression of the trade by England and France, and it was partly to watch this traffic that a British consul was posted to Bahia, although the town also accommodated many English merchants at the time (Verger 1964).

What immediately impressed observers was the careful planning behind the rising. The first report of the British consul, J. Parkinson, was sent to the Duke of Wellington on the following day (26 January 1835). He spoke of the role of the Nago blacks, "who comprise the chief part of the slave population of the city." He went on to say that "it was widely extended and combined with far greater ability than is usual in such affairs."[6]

Incendiary fires were lit in several parts of the city. Simultaneous attacks were made on the guard at the palace, the cavalry quarters, and the barracks of the artillery, *caçadores,* and national and municipal troops.

Three days later Parkinson wrote again with more information. The revolt had been planned for daybreak, "when household slaves are despatched for water and their masters and mistresses are engaged in Church devotions" (the twenty-fifth of that month was a Sunday). Most of the *brancos* (whites) were in the suburb of Bomfim on an annual pilgrimage to the church of Nossa Senhora da Guia, where they were particularly vulnerable to attack (Kent 1970: 350–51). According to one commentator, the great opportunity of the rebels was lost owing to impetuosity, for the rising started three hours too early, losing the advantage of coordinated timing. In fact, the authorities had been warned by two Yoruba women, ex-slaves, who announced before 10 P.M. on the twenty-fourth that an insurrection was about to take place. As a result of this information, the soldiers forced an entry into a building owned by two of the participants, the ex-slaves Belchior and Caspar. This house was one of two meeting places, each with its own Muslim religious instructor, in this case Luiz Sanim, of Nupe origin. The other group, from the Victoria quarter, consisted mainly of slaves working for Englishmen; they met in a "straw" house where there was a religious school under the supervision of one Thomas, a slave. When the soldiers attacked the first meeting place, they surprised some sixty armed blacks, who overpowered them and then directed their attack against the main centers of Brazilian power. At that time this was the army barracks, but today in West Africa the radio station, that focus of communication, is usually one of the first targets in any coup.

Nina Rodrigues described the role of Islam in Bahia at that period, which had been brought there by captured Hausa and later by other Muslims (which Rodrigues called "Tapa," that is, Nupe as well as Yoruba).[7] He connected these uprisings with the famous jihad, or holy war, proclaimed by Uthman dan Fodio in 1804 against the infidel in northern Nigeria, which led to the conquest of the Hausa, Nupe, and northern Yoruba and to the present dominance of the Fulani ruling elite. These slaves, he noted, were not uncivilized natives but members of warrior cultures who knew how to read and write Arabic script (Rodrigues 1932). Indeed, according to the historian Freyre, the standard of literacy of the Muslim population was greater than that of most of the white colonists—some of them illiterate, most of them semiliterate, almost none being capable of signing their names. These Africans did not easily take on the role of simple cultivators or accept forced baptism into the Christian faith. One should add that in South America in the first half of the nineteenth century, unlike many other slave societies, there was continual communication with Africa back and forth across the Atlantic, in which Brazil played a dominant role. Not only did each slave shipment bring news of the homeland, but blacks were involved in the trade itself and established "Brazilian" settlements along the Guinea coast, while free Africans even made the voyage to South America. Contact with the world of Islam was maintained in a minor way, just as Yoruba cults, especially after the end of the slave trade, were reinforced by visits and by consultations between the two continents.[8]

In Bahia many slaves were employed as palanquin bearers, often by nonlocal whites, and especially by the English, whose servants were suspected by the local whites of complicity during the major revolt of 1835. These Protestant masters were presumably less concerned with the commitment of their charges to the Catholic faith and may have encouraged incipient signs of literate activity. Two participants in the revolt took refuge in the house of the British vice-consul, who happened to be the consul's son-in-law, and were instantly "surrendered," but in other cases the merchants claimed "British privilege" for the runaways, who "were pertinaciously harboured . . . in defiance of law civil and military." The local whites resented this assumption of privilege and openly charged the British, whose activities were regarded with great hostility, "with inciting their own slaves to insurrection and preparing them to emulate the horrors of San Domingo" (Rodrigues 1965; Parkinson to Wellington, 29 January 1835).

Rodrigues's analysis of the 1835 revolt was based mainly on the report of the chief of police, later governor, Francisco Gonçalves Martins, who explained how the rebellion "had been planned over a longer period, in utmost secrecy and in a way that was not to be expected from brutish and ignorant beings. In general, all knew how to write and read in unknown characters resembling the Arabic used by the Hausa which now appears to have spread to the Yorubas [who had largely replaced the Hausa, whom they had joined in previous revolts]. They had some educated people who gave lessons and tried to organize the insurrection in which freed Africans [that is, blacks born in Africa] and even some rich ones, were involved." He found many books that they claimed contained religious precepts drawn from the Qur'an. Certainly religion had a part in this revolt, even at the level of the leaders telling "these poor people that these papers could protect them from death."[9]

Of the writings referred to by Rodrigues, some have apparently been lost. What have remained seem to be mainly religious (Monteil 1967; Reichert 1967; Reichert and Abdelghani 1966). However, a resumé of other materials was made by a Hausa named Albino and written in Arabic characters (Rodrigues 1932: 105–6; Verger 1968: 341). According to this source, some of these papers contained instructions to the insurgents coming from the Victoria quarter to seize the country, kill all the whites, and then go to a meeting place where they would be joined by people from the interior.[10] Other papers were designed to protect the rebels from the bullets of police and soldiers. One, signed by a Mala Abubakar, that is, by a *mallam* or learned man, was a kind of proclamation, exhorting the people to unite and asserting that nothing would harm them on the way. We may contrast this mode of gathering a group together with the "drumbeats" and "nocturnal ritual gatherings" used in the revolt in Saint-Domingue in August 1781 (Parry and Sherlock 1965: 163). The author, Mallam Abubakar, may have been the imam, that is, the religious leader, at the time of the revolt, although this was apparently unknown to the police and only told to Rodrigues much later by a subsequent imam; nevertheless, the *mallam* was later expelled to Africa along with many others (Verger 1968: 349). Another letter was sent from one Allei to Adao, slave of an Englishman, saying he would arrive at 4 A.M. and Adao should not leave without him—a message presumably referring to the planned attack at daybreak. Finally, the searches revealed an ABC and writing boards used for teaching the written language.

Documents had also been discovered after the projected revolt of 1807, which started as a result of an attempt to suppress the nearby *quilambos* by breaking off their relationship with the town. This earlier rising was definitely attributed to the Hausa, though some Mandinka continuing "fanaticism," a hatred toward whites and Christians. While they could not read Arabic (using instead a Portuguese translation of the Qur'an) and employed Yoruba as a lingua franca, the structure of the community was fully Islamic, with an imam, muezzin, and alkali. They regretted they had no mosque, but they observed prayers and the five pillars of Islam; used a lunar calendar for the festivals; avoided pork, fermented drink, and animal blood; and consumed the ink with which *surahs* of the Qur'an had been written on boards (known as *wala uassa*).[12]

The strength of Islam in Bahia at the time of the revolt had been considerable. "The atmosphere that preceded the movement of '35 in Bahia was one of intense religious ardour among the slaves. In Mata-Porcos Lane on the Praça slopes, at St. Francis' Cross, in the very shadow of the Catholic churches and monasteries," writes Freyre, ". . . slaves who were schooled in the Koran preached the religion of the Prophet, setting it over against the religion of Christ that was followed by their masters, up above in the Big Houses. They propagandized against the Catholic Mass, saying that it was the same as worshipping a stick of wood; and to the Christian rosary with its cross of Our Lord they opposed their own" (1946: 315).[13]

While Islam later had to go underground for a while, Freyre notes its continuing influence on Brazilian Christianity, with its prayer-papers to deliver the body from death (Freyre 1946: 316). The position taken by some blacks and coloreds toward Protestantism may be related to these earlier anti-Catholic prejudices. Moreover, various rituals seem to smack of Islam, such as a feast of the dead in Penedo, with its long prayers and fasting, abstinence from alcohol, lunar calendar, long white tunics, and sacrifice of a sheep.

In his observations of African practices in Pernambuco (he too calls them "sects") Freyre noted how people removed their shoes at ceremonies, avoided treading on an old mat, crossed their legs, passed around colored cloths while dancing, and drank the ink washed off writing boards. "In this way the Catholicism of the Big Houses was enriched with Musulman influences" (Freyre 1946: 318).

Some 800 blacks took part in the uprising of 1835, in which 14 lost their lives. Three hundred twenty-six persons were arrested, including were also arrested (Kent 1970: 343, 349). The same group appears to have been involved in the revolts of 1808, 1809, and 1814. However, those of 1826 and 1830 were mainly Yoruba (though Dahomeans are also mentioned), and the 1809 rising was blamed on the Yoruba secret society called Ogboni, which Kent saw as one possible reason why it was undetected; that made it a unique case, for in the other instances some informer always succumbed to the reward that was being offered by the authorities.

In the discussions of the later revolt we find references to the role of Muslim schools, to marabouts or *alufas* as well as to the *limano* (imam) (Rodrigues 1932: 54); more recently, from 1900, we encounter descriptions of the observance of the annual Muslim fast, of mosques, of gris-gris (talismans), of washing the writing from tablets and drinking the liquid (Rodrigues 1932: 68). No one can doubt the importance of Islam in nineteenth-century Brazil, despite the fact that after the revolt of 1835 an effort was made to deport back to Africa all freed blacks who could read and write. That truly draconian measure was aimed at depriving the blacks of their literate members, a move that hit the Muslim community hard.[11] A ban was placed on "unorthodox cults"; subversives and undesirables were expelled to West Africa, four hundred in all, while slaves received a hundred lashes. Some of those who could go voluntarily did so, with about eight hundred passports being issued between October and December 1837. This return of the learned (as well as the watchfulness of the police) seems to have taken the heart out of further revolt. In any case Islam was partly driven underground, although groups such as Candomble that attempted to combine Catholicism and Islam or Yoruba cults were allowed to flourish. Syncretism was safe.

There certainly appears to have been a falling off in commitment to Islam after 1835, partly because of suppression, partly because of syncretic adjustment. Nevertheless, a tradition of Islam continued, as we see clearly from Etienne's 1909 study of the revolt. His general knowledge of the "sect"—he used the term to define what he considered to be a special Brazilian version of Islam—was derived from Muslims he talked to at the beginning of the twentieth century, including Imam Hassoumanou, imam of all Brazil, a resident in Bahia. He observed a

26 women; 286 participated in the nine-year trial, 120 of them free blacks. Of the leaders (all African-born), 7 were free, 4 slaves; 10 were Yoruba, 1 was Hausa, and 1 was Nupe. Of the 160 slaves accused, 50 were employed by strangers, 45 of them by the English; 52 were domestic servants, 37 were palanquin bearers, and 33 were street traders and store clerks.[14] A number of them appear to have formed a club to learn the Qur'an, including José, a Yoruba who was found with papers, and João, another Yoruba employed by an Englishman, who had not only papers but guns. Many of the slaves in Bahia appear to have been *negros de ganho,* who worked independently but turned over an agreed percentage of their weekly earnings to their masters (Kent 1970: 340). Aruna (Haruna, a Yoruba with a Muslim name) sold water; Sule (Suleman, though Victoria was his Christian name) sold cloth.[15] Licutan, a Yoruba slave known as Pacifico, was one of the leaders and could read and write; the Hausa Dandara sold tobacco. The Yoruba Luiz and Gaspar were tailors, as was José from the Congo; Ahora, a freed Yoruba, carried lime; Dada was a smith; Namomin, a Yoruba, worked with a butcher.

All had entered various trades, and none was a plantation hand. Sanim (the Nupe leader also known as Luiz) organized a kind of *esusu,* a friendly society, providing rotating credit by collecting the contributions of its members in order to buy their freedom and purchase clothes;[16] the purchase of freedom was common enough throughout Latin America, the provision of loans being one of the functions of the black fraternities *(irmandade* or *confraria),* the most important of which was Our Lady of the Rosary, founded by the Dominicans and established in Portugal in the fifteenth century for the defense, conversion, and control of slaves.[17] The fraternity, whose officers had to be freed blacks and its scribe a white of noble birth, was also concerned with participation in processions, with providing proper burials, and with representing its members in lawsuits against their masters.

The variety of documents obtained from the participants in the revolt shows that we are not dealing simply with writing for magical charms, nor even with writing for religious uses alone. In the first place, the fact that writing was employed in the uprising to make secret arrangements by means of letters suggests that the superior planning was partly related to literacy. Second, the magical power of the word (and the book), as manifest in the use of *surahs* of the Qur'an sewn into leather pouches on coats, was directed to secular aims, being thought to protect the wearer from the enemy's weapons. Indeed, in northern Nigeria during this period the leather pouches, like the quilted kapok coats of the horsemen, helped to deflect the arrows of enemy archers.[18] Such protective medicines against firearms were not the exclusive possession of Islam (Genovese 1981: 47). They were sold, for example, by Akan Obeahmen in Jamaica in 1760 (Schuler 1970: 383) and by the LoDagaa in northern Ghana in 1900 (Goody 1956). I do not mean to suggest these were all derivative from Islam. But the belief in the efficacy of these *madingas,* known in West Africa as *safi,* against the bullets of the white man—a belief also found in the 1807 revolt (Rodrigues 1932)—was a matter not only of magical power or material protection but of religious faith. A somewhat similar use of writing was found in the practice whereby an individual drank the ink washed off the wooden tablets on which *surahs* of the Qur'an had been written. Rodrigues quotes Binger's reference to the practice in Timbuctu, but it also occurred widely in North Africa and throughout the Muslim world as well as among the ancient Hebrews as a kind of ordeal.

Third, the written religion of Islam appears to have provided some kind of ideological backing to the revolt. Although an obvious feature of the protests of African slaves, the notion of "death to the whites" is very characteristic of many twentieth-century uprisings in West Africa, where a widely used word for "white," *nasala,* is derived from the Arabic form of *Nazarene,* "Christian" (Goody 1970, 1982). Ethnic and even racial definitions were again dominated by religious ones.

Fourth, writing may in fact have helped people to gain their freedom because of the contribution it enabled them to make to the work of their masters (often semi-independent work), and then to remain free once they had done so. Somewhat later, about 1848, the French consul at Bahia, François de Castelnau, tried to question a Muslim called Mohammad-Abdullad Filani (Fulani) who had been living there for some thirty years and had liberated himself by his work as a carpenter. He could read and write not only in his own language but in Portuguese. According to de Castelnau, he remained "very intolerant and fanatic," even trying to convert the consul to Islam. When the Frenchman offered him money to come and work for him, Filani turned to another black and declared that he did not want to serve a Christian dog. This man of seventy, a marabout, claimed to have made the voyage to Mecca. He was born in Kano and was taken prisoner at Katsina by the Hausa during the Fulani wars. In his discussions he returned constantly to the faith of Mohammad, which was the basis of all, and the only thing in this world worthy of occupying a man's time (Verger 1968: 327–28).

It is amazing to consider that Mohammad-Abdullad had been to Mecca and back, then to the New World, while the imam, Abubakar, traveled because of his faith from Nigeria to Brazil and back again. Other Africans in Brazil, whether Muslims or not, did not lose contact with their former homeland, the Yoruba continuing to import religious rituals for personal use, as well as kola nuts, cowries, soap, striped indigo, cloth, and palm oil. Down to the end of the nineteenth century Hausa and Yoruba freedmen from Bahia were being repatriated to Africa, some of them founding Porto Seguiro, in Ardra, as well as other settlements. A delegation of Quakers that visited Rio in 1852 was received by a commission of freedmen from the province of Minas Gerais, seventy of whom had been repatriated to Benin. They presented the English visitors with documents written in Arabic (Candler and Burgess 1853; Freyre 1946: 318).

The words of Mohammad-Abdullad run counter to widely held notions about the syncretism of African religions, about adaptation to the forms of Christianity or of slave society. In West Africa and elsewhere Islam was constantly making compromises with local beliefs; this was one of the ostensible causes of the Fulani-Hausa wars, for the family of Uthman dan Fodio was highly literate and aimed at introducing a purer version of Islam, that is, going back to the Book (Last 1967). But here we find a statement of a firm follower of the movements of reform generated by the Fulani, a man convinced of his particular faith and unwilling to compromise that faith in any way. As Rodrigues notes, the revolt was defined in religious rather than tribal terms; Muslims participated regardless of ethnic group, although the latter affiliations were still of considerable importance. The strength of these insurrections has been attributed to the religious organization, to the propaganda and to the teaching of Islam. In planning, execution, and defeat, religion sustained the morale of the rebels. "The moral greatness that certain insurgents showed in the face of danger and death, was the real key to these insurrections which had nothing to do with the despair of slavery," for the richer ones took part and non-Muslims were excluded (Verger 1968: 349–50).

The British representative at Rio, whose name was Fox, also praised "the personal boldness which they displayed"; indeed, this and the "extensive system of combination" that preceded the rising were seen to give "just cause of alarm," and he notes that "the intelligence of this revolt has spread more uneasiness in Rio de Janeiro, than any other public disturbance which has occurred for many years" (Fox to Wellington, 11 February 1835 [FO 13/117]). At the same time Fox considered the black insurgents not to have had "any definite object in view, beyond burning and plundering, and murdering at random; or not to have any distinct notion of freeing themselves from slavery." On this subject his opinion ran directly counter to that of the local chief of police, later to be governor.[19]

According to Genovese, throughout the Americas "Muslim slaves earned a reputation for being especially rebellious" (1981: 29). While African cults provided an ideological rallying point for certain revolts (Obeahmen, Myalmen, Vodûn priests, Ñáñigos), Muslims led the great uprisings in Saint-Domingue and in Surinam, despite their numerical insignificance. Macendal, leader of the most important early resistance movement in Saint-Domingue, has been described as a Muslim, while Boukman, leader of the rising that sparked off the great revolt itself, was a Vodûn priest (Genovese 1981: 86). And presumably Islam was involved in the early rising of the Wolofs on Hispaniola in 1522; as a result, in 1532 the Spanish forbade the importation of Wolofs to America because of their reputation for insubordination and rebelliousness. Mulatto slaves became the next target, their entry being forbidden in 1543 because many were suspected of Moorish ancestry and therefore of exposure to Islam. Berber and Moorish slaves had already been excluded in 1506 because of possible Islamic faith, although, as in the other cases, such laws were mostly ineffective (Bowser 1974: 148, 360).

In his general account of slave revolts in the Americas Genovese (1981) proposes a progression from rebellion to revolution, a pattern of protest similar to that discussed for other parts of the world (for example, Gluckman 1955a). This shift he sees as roughly corresponding to the transition from seigneurialism to capitalism. In the early period, he argues, revolts were basically forms of withdrawal from society, restorationist in character, attempting to relocate African village life in the colonial setting. The change came with the bourgeois-democratic influence of the French Revolution and its cries of *"liberté, egalité, et fraternité,"* reaching its high point with the overthrow of the whites in Haiti in 1791, after which nothing was the same.

This periodization of slave revolts seems overdetermined, if only because it does not allow sufficiently for the role of another literate creed, Islam. Moreover, slavery was to disappear for a variety of reasons (one of which, as in Brazil, was certainly rebellion), while liberty was no less an aim of the early movements of protest. It is true that the cries of liberty and equality were raised by a nationalist political movement in Bahia in 1798 under the possible influence of the French Revolution (Kent 1970: 336–37). But well before this, in 1692, "Death to the whites and long live liberty" had been the battle cry of a *mocambo* in the Bahia captaincy. Like most such communities, this settlement was situated near the towns and farms on which it depended. In active communication with the town, often through taverns, the runaways lived not by agriculture but parasitically by highway robbery, cattle rustling, raiding, and extortion (Schwartz 1970: 322). While some African villages may have had a similar mode of livelihood, it was certainly not the norm, and the reaction here seems to have been less a matter of the restoration of rural life than of escape and survival. Above all, the African-derived religion of Islam provided an ideology that focused the resistance to domination by Christian whites.

The proclamations of the French Revolution displayed a characteristic feature of written creeds; like the Declaration of the Rights of Man and of the Citizen, they were universalistic, generalized, indeed overgeneralized. For the Girondins, for Napoleon, and to some extent for Toussaint-Louverture himself, all men were to be equal, free, brothers—ideals that inevitably had to compromise with the reality of circumstances, certainly after victory had been achieved. But the written creed was important in providing an explicit ideology for getting rid of a social order that did not measure up to the wishes of the oppressed. Islam played a similar role, even if its creed was directed as much to the other world as to this. Individual leaders of revolts were often literate despite the fact that the bulk of the participants were not.

Of the major uprisings in the United States—those of Gabriel Prosser in 1800, Denmark Vesey in 1822, and Nat Turner in 1831—all the leaders "had learned to read and write and had special talents and privileges" (Genovese 1981: 44). Significantly, after all these revolts there were "restrictions on literacy, preaching, manumission, and much else" (Genovese 1981: 113). The main leader of the Haitian struggle, Toussaint-Louverture, had read and been much influenced by the abolitionist Abbé Raynal's *Philosophical and Political History of the Establishments and Commerce of the Europeans in the Two Indies,* the first French edition of which was published in 1775 (James 1938: 16). But if literacy made its mark in revolts inspired by European declarations, it also played its part in quite a different tradition, that of Islam, which rejected the rule of those who did not follow a different book, the Qur'an, whether in West Africa or in Brazil. And the results of its commitment to literacy were particularly marked in the Bahia revolt of 1835.

I want to try to generalize from these observations and ask to what extent the effects of Islam were due not to Islam in itself but to the fact that it was a Religion of the Book. Written religions, taken as a whole, have some general characteristics that make them differ from the generality of oral religions, and these in turn have a bearing upon the role of Islam in Bahia.

First, however, I want to refer to another aspect of this situation. There is always a problem in talking about societies with and without writing in terms of the oral and literate traditions because any society with writing obviously uses both channels and there are differences between individuals and between subgroups in their competence and performance in one or the other. Some individuals may never use the written channel at all, and these we speak of as illiterates. But their position, activities, and knowledge will differ in significant respects from those of members of truly nonliterate societies, since illiterates will be defined (and will define themselves) in opposition to the dominant literate mode. Nor is this simply a question of self-definition in the general sense beloved by social scientists. The oral tradition of popular culture is influenced not only by juxtaposition, but in content, conceptually, by the written tradition. Of course, this influence is a matter of degree. The practices of some Indians in Brazil and Mexico were altered very early on by the insistence of the regular clergy, especially the Jesuits, on obedience to European-derived marriage and other restrictions that could transform their lives. Others were influenced very little. But these influences might also vary over time. Within the slave community in Bahia in the early part of the last century, the *orixas* (from *oria*, Yoruba for "gods") seem to be of secondary importance, at least in a political context, with their practitioners standing in opposition, even subordination, to the leaders of the Hausa, Nupe, and Yoruba Muslims. The consequences, both for Catholic syncretism and for the later preeminence of the *orixas,* of sending away most of the literate Muslims is an interesting question of cultural history. Did one rise as the other fell, or rise in a more adaptationist, less literate, mold? As Prince (1972) has argued, with Islam and "unorthodox cults" being forced underground, the time for eclecticism was at hand. Indeed, syncretism appears to have had the encouragement of the authorities.

In looking at the specific features of written religions that may have influenced the situation in Bahia, let us recall that when we speak of religion in an oral culture, we do so with reference to a population boundary, whether it be tribe or nation. Asante religion or Ojibway religion is what that particular group practices at a particular place and time. Written religions, on the other hand, are defined in relation to a text; while not all are Religions of the Book (in the sense of the alphabetic religions of the Near East), they all have texts to which reference is made. Consequently we define the religion in nonethnic terms, that is, as Christian or Hindu, and the religion is capable of crossing tribal or national boundaries and hence of recruiting adherents, as in the Bahia revolt, on a nontribal basis—of overcoming, in this respect, the tribal divisions that the Brazilian owners and some of the slaves themselves attempted to preserve.

But because written religions, especially alphabetic ones, cross tribal boundaries while oral ones do not, that does not imply that the latter are fixed and static while the former are infinitely malleable. Rather, it is the opposite. The fact that we speak of Asante or LoDagaa religion does not mean that these sets of practices and beliefs are the same today as they were yesterday, much less the day before that.[20]

I have argued that quite the opposite is true, that because African religions are closely linked to matters of health and well-being, they are inevitably more open-ended, if only because they are constantly faced with the problem of the God that failed, the unsuccessful cure, the promise made but unfulfilled. The closer the entailment of religious activity with the affairs of daily life, that is, the greater the contextualization, the more often the problem will arise. Consequently, I argue that truth is not fixed, as if residing in an immutable text, but involves a constant search, a seeking, a quest, after new solutions to old problems.

Only by some such hypothesis can I explain the changing face of, say, LoDagaa religion in partial contrast to Islam. While it has its fixed points in the shape of the heavens (the High God, the mystical aspect of the sky), the Earth (the mystical aspect of the land and soil), and the ancestors (the mystical aspect of humanity), there is an intermediary area in which lesser gods or shrines have a rather high degree of turnover. Some rise in popularity while others fall, like recipients of votive offerings. Nor are such new gods always of internal creation. For example, from northern Ghana several so-called medicine shrines spread far and wide throughout West Africa. While the extent and rapidity of the spread was partly due to new modes of transport and the more active networks of personal communication, the phenomenon itself was not new. Movement had always occurred.

The turnover of adherents to the cult of Nana Brukung, outside its home area of Shiare in the Togo hills of West Africa, was high (Pollock 1979). Clients and client groups come and go, although some supplicants have established the shrine in their own locality. Indeed, the cult was taken to South America and is incorporated into Afro-Brazilian religion today (Soyinka 1990). Attachment to such shrines often oscillates like the upsurge and downturn of people attending the church of a specific saint, as with the contemporary attachment to the Church of

São Judeus Thaddeus in São Paulo (another cult that crossed the Atlantic). By migration the cult activities get incorporated in the cosmological, classificatory, and sacrificial systems of other groups, changing in subtle ways the nature of these cultures. Nor can we argue that this change is superficial even if limited. The notion that what changes is surface structure and what continues is deep is an idea to which many anthropologists and others subscribe, especially in the earlier America of themes and Ruth Benedict; it has had many more recent rebirths but always embodies a tautology that distracts from intellectual inquiry by assuming what needs to be proven. It is not always false, but it may be profoundly mistaken (another way of putting it is that the truth-value is of truth by fiat, by definition).

The invocation of the Bagre myth of the LoDagaa lists the main concerns of man as farming, chicken raising, hunting, and childbirth. Religion—especially, in this context, dealing with health and well-being—involves an active search, not only among existing agencies by means of the diviner (who is supposed to seek the truth, *yilmiong,* but may be lying or more usually mistaken, though the LoDagaa do not always make a clear distinction between these aspects of nontruth) but also among other agencies, new shrines, revealed by the beings of the wild. Life is a quest, a journey. The myth of the Bagre traces the journey of one of the first two men, in the course of which humanity acquires culture: the ability to make iron hoes and arrows, then to farm and fight, copulate and cook, and make beer (this last being lengthily described).

It is interesting that in the recitation of the Bagre the High God and the beings of the wild play the dominant roles, to the virtual exclusion of the ancestors (whom, of course, the first men had to do without) and of medicine shrines, indeed, even of the Earth itself. So if one were to write down this recitation and look upon it as an inclusive statement of LoDagaa religion or cosmology, as might happen in the early stages of literacy, one would be greatly deceived—deceived in the sense that a large number of other, very central ritual activities are excluded, especially those to do with the Earth shrine and the ancestors, who are minimally incorporated in the myth and who are perhaps more oriented toward action (or deed) than toward the verbal. That is not altogether the right way of putting it. The ancestors receive endless prayers and supplications, but they are not placed in a narrative context nor in a structured, pantheon-type relationship with other agencies. Indeed, regular pantheons are rare in West African religions, apart from Dahomey and Yoruba, for the development of such a frame is another general tendency of writing.

There is a further deception involved in transcribing the myth. By writing down a version of the Bagre, one crystallizes a particular recitation, creating text from utterance. The use of a particular version for analysis presents no worries if one is comforted by the thought (a thought encouraged by the absence of any other transcriptions or anthropologists) that all possible versions are identical (the fallacy of the single case) or that all possible versions are simply transformations of basic themes, principles, structures (which is a fallacy of structural-functional analysis). My own evidence proclaims the difficulties, if not the impossibility, of reproducing long utterances in a verbatim fashion in oral cultures and suggests that the variations mean we have to allow for syntagmatic change in important elements in the structure. That is, unless structure is defined in a tautologous way by what is common to a set, the lowest common denominator of elementary arithmetic, it must be allowed that the written version of an oral recitation transforms one of many possible performances into a fixed text. That fixed text then has to be taken into account in future performances or exegesis. The notion of a fixed text presents a conceptual difficulty to some (Parry 1984; Fuller 1984). It is not that the text is incapable of different interpretations—that is only too obvious. But as we saw with the Fulani jihad, under a very wide range of circumstances the text remains a continuing source of interpretation that may conflict with current "compromises" or assertions. Reference to the fixed text lay behind the ideological inspiration of the Fulani movement, whose leaders were learned men, writers as well as readers, just as it had lain behind that other great back-to-the-Book movement, Protestantism. Protestantism crystallized around another significant change in the modes of communication that ushered in printing and made the text directly available to a much greater number of people than was possible in any manuscript culture. Manuscript cultures had encouraged the continuing importance of the spoken version of the written word, of reading aloud and recitation. And it encouraged the verbatim internalization of the written word that we find so well illustrated in the mnemonic techniques of the Arabic school and the swallowing of the word by washing the written text off the tablet and drinking it.

The fixing of a text necessarily involves the selection, the almost accidental selection, of one oral version at one time and at one place. Looked at in a long-range perspective, the definitive shift to literate forms puts an end to the creative development of particular long oral recitations (though it opens up other possibilities). Even in mixed situations, problems arise. The Bagre that I first recorded and published has for at least some of the schooled population become the authorized version; the text, as opposed to the utterance, is orthodox. And it is authoritative not only because it is written but because it was written earlier and taken down from ancestral figures now departed. As such, it has become a standard version in a way no oral version could be.

The main point to which I wanted to draw attention, however, has to do with content. If one's view of LoDagaa religion rested upon this written version of the Bagre, it would be much more theocentric than is given by the total picture of religious action and belief. It also leans more toward a picture of the universe that, if not monotheistic, at least emphasizes God's role.

In suggesting why this should be so, one is on difficult ground. But because the myth deals with the creation of the world, or rather of culture, it tends to emphasize the unique source of the unique act. If the myth had been more directly concerned with healing, then the emphasis might perhaps have been on the plurality of the saints (or shrines) rather than on the uniqueness of God. And saints, like ancestors, are by definition nonscriptural, or rather postscriptural. If we go back to the Book, we eliminate them, though by so doing we may create a gap in our understanding of the world. That argument suggests one kind of possible explanation for the tendency of written religions to emphasize the uniqueness of the godhead.

In practice Islam, like Christianity, treads a fine line between the concept of the one God and the recognition of other agencies, such as the jinn, the equivalent of the beings of the wild of the Bagre. But since the jinn are not scriptural, they get swept aside from time to time by reform movements of the Fulani kind that inevitably adopt the so-called intolerance encountered by de Castelnau in his interview with Mohammad-Abdullad at Bahia in 1848, or by Etienne fifty years later.

Intolerance is connected with universalism. Not all literate religions are necessarily universalistic, but they have tendencies in that direction, if only because their commandments tend to get phrased in somewhat decontextualized, that is, universalistic, ways. The establishment of the universal church necessarily excludes other views, for religion is no longer defined politically (as is LoDagaa religion) but theologically, in fact scripturally, by writing. It can spread independently of political institutions, although political support, however temporary, often helps. And it emerges in opposition ("Thou shalt have no other gods but me"), hence giving birth to a boundary between Jew and Gentile, but more strongly between Christian and pagan (pagans were also "gentiles" in the early letters of Jesuit fathers from Brazil), or between Muslim and infidel *(kaffir)*. The terms used are often ones of abuse, frequently with animal implications, such as "Christian dog," "*kaffir* son of a bitch," or "pagan swine," making it perhaps easier to despise them, spit upon them, stone them, even kill them if they refuse to be converted.

To return finally to Brazil, there are two other points that are linked to the means of communication and the Bahia revolt. The first has to do with the problem of conversion. You cannot convert to an oral religion—you become a member of the political system (a "tribe") and you subscribe, to a greater or lesser degree, to the beliefs of the group. Conversion implies a different definition of religion, commitment to a fixed text (beliefs or rituals), and it involves giving up one set of practices and beliefs in favor of another. Hence Islam was able to crosscut ethnic affiliations.

Second, the existence of conversion, of supratribal recruitment, means that the religion must necessarily break out of its local bonds; it must become partly decontextualized and partly universalized. Now, while these are preconditions for the spread of a multitribal religion, they are also part of the implications of literacy itself. That is to say, with writing, moral injunctions and jural norms tend to get phrased in a more generalized way than when these injunctions or norms are embedded in action situations. We find statements such as "Thou shalt not kill" rather than "Thou shalt not kill anyone (a) except those who are themselves killers (Law of Talio) (b) except non-Jews (c) except in times of war," and so on. Such generalized norms in one sense create the notion of the brotherhood of man by making it explicit. But the presence of these (literate) ideals also raises problems, since in practice, in context, compromise is forced upon the community. The result is an increased measure of cognitive dissonance, of conflict between ideal and "reality," which produces dissent groups consisting of those who take the generalized norm (for example, against killing) more literally (to the letter) than do others.

I have tried to point out some of the general tendencies of written religions that seemed relevant to a set of revolts in nineteenth-century Brazil. Those revolts themselves provide a contrast with West Africa, where the percentage of slaves in some states was probably as great as in Brazil (that is, some 50 percent) but where, although fear was expressed about slave risings, these were few and far between. The reasons are several, but in West Africa the oppressed did not, unlike earlier Christians, have a book to guide, sustain, and stimulate them to revolt. As with the non-Muslim slaves in Brazil, residual tribal affiliation led to greater disunity, which was then exploited by the masters, who encouraged personal dependence and religious collegiality ("We are all Muslims [or Christians] now"). This cultural pattern was altered by the influence of writing, in regard to both the short-term influence of the technology and the long-term influence of what is stored and developed.

I have taken a specific example of the role of writing in a language that was understood by only a few during a revolt of blacks in nineteenth-century Brazil, the comparative success of which has been attributed to writing and to a written religion. Its very success resulted in the dispatch of many of those able to read and write back to the Africa from which they came, since, as elsewhere, the authorities feared underdogs who were literate.

Using as an implicit contrast the religion of an oral society, the LoDagaa, I have pointed out some general features of written religions that might have accompanied the recruitment of insurgents from a number of tribes, for written religions tend to be differently defined by reference to fixed texts, not politically but theologically. Such texts may provide relatively fixed points of reference not only for ritual and myth but also for beliefs and moral injunctions. That is to say, obviously morality has to be embodied in a particular place and time, but inevitably it has to be partially decontextualized and universalized, then subsequently re-contextualized in a particular situation, such as a text when it is read or recited. These characteristics, often remarked upon in literacy studies, are attributes not only of written religion but of written communication itself, for writing employs only a single channel (instead of the many involved in speech) and is usually aimed at a wider, more distant, and more impersonal audience.[21]

6
Derrida among the Archives
of the Written and the Oral

The theme of this book runs against certain trends in French poststructuralist discussions. In that context the very division into oral and written may sound like the invention of structuralist binarism (which is to be rejected), an instance of the great divide. In fact, the premise is incorrect: Writing is one of many discriminations needed to discuss changes (and differences) in the modes of communication, the highly significant shift from gesture to language being basic to the human situation and that from manuscript to printing cultures basic to modernity. Each of these changes (differences) alters the nature of the storage and archiving of information. Gesture can be copied, but it can be recorded only by the visual memory (and sometimes by the tactile). Speech requires the verbal memory store. With writing, one no longer needs to stock all one's possible information internally; all that is necessary is an idea of how to get at it, as in, say, the *Larousse* or *Petit Robert*. This provides a multitude of opportunities that cannot exist with speech alone.

When I entitled my 1987 book *The Interface between the Written and the Oral,* that phrase was meant to be understood at several levels. First, there is the historical level. Writing was invented by human beings at a particular moment in time, so historically (as well as in the recent past) we have societies that are purely oral and societies that have added writing. Put in this way, it might sound as though we were dealing with an exclusive opposition and could talk of orality versus literacy. But the change is not the replacement formerly envisaged in the shift from one mode of production to another, with feudalism substituting for the slavery of ancient society, or capitalism replacing feudalism (indeed, even those absolute progressions are now often modified by the notion of articulation or else are in part abandoned). Oral communication obviously continues to play a fundamental role after the advent of writing, just as writing continues to be fundamental with the advent of the electronic media. While people talk freely of the disappearance of the book, such talk is loose and unsustainable. Before you can put the *Larousse* on a CD-ROM you have to organize the material in writing, then type or scan it into the computer, and finally read it.

At a societal level there is an interface between societies with writing (that is, literate) and those without it (that is, nonliterate or preliterate). Contrary to the view of the hierarchy proposed by Derrida, the written is virtually always considered the superior, even by neighboring oral cultures. Hence the rapidity of the shift to literacy, especially over the last hundred years. Once introduced, writing rarely fades away, rarely undergoes the process that W. H. R. Rivers described as "the disappearance of useful arts" (1912).

Again, there is the interface between readers and nonreaders within the same society—not literates and nonliterates, but literates and illiterates. This division, a hierarchy, dominated the history of post–Bronze Age societies from 3000 B.C.E. to the nineteenth century. It is reflected in the split between high and low culture as well as in a variety of dimensions of differentiation, of stratification, of styles of life, and has been fundamental to the history of all "advanced" societies.

Finally, there is the interface in each one of us between our performance in the written register and our performance in the oral one. We all know people, including some great teachers, who speak much better than they write. There are others more facile in the written, such as the English poet Thomas Gray, who wrote "Elegy in a Country Churchyard" and of whom it was said he was a fool when he spoke but an angel when he wrote.

These levels of distinction between the written and the spoken have been played down by some, including Derrida, who sees them as part of the "logocentric" character of the philosophical tradition (though it is difficult to see how humans, who are essentially language-using animals, can be anything but logocentric). Derrida starts from the observation, correct in my opinion, that those who write about language have privileged speech over writing and presented them as a hierarchy. He concentrates on Saussure and Rousseau. Saussure had seen writing simply as a means of representing speech, a representation of a representation. Writing thus becomes a distortion of speech, a bastard form of communication, as much earlier Plato had seen it. In making this hierarchical judgment about speech and writing, Plato started the logocentric tradition of European philosophy, a tradition from which Derrida finds it impossible to escape; it is possible only to reveal the internal contradictions that prevent it from becoming a coherent system, that is, to deconstruct the whole notion. Saussure takes a simpler view about speech; however, he does see it as being infected by the "tyranny of writing," so that writing is not simply dependent on speech but affects it, supplements it.

These trends, Derrida maintains, have influenced Western philosophy toward "logocentricism" and the metaphysics of presence, which, as we see, he can challenge but not escape. He disputes the notion that reality is made up of a series of present states, *cogito ergo sum,* since in fact every moment is marked by traces of the past and future (to which the arrow flies). There is a crucial sense in which these differences of time, these tenses, are always present.

However, even in 1967, when Derrida was writing, it was not always true that speech was given priority. He does not seem to be aware of the body of work (for example, of the Toronto School of Innes, McLuhan, Havelock, and others) that has studied writing and the differences it made to human life and thought. It is a characteristic of much modern philosophical discourse (although it was not always thus and philosophers are not alone in it) that a philosopher sees himself able to approach a topic without inquiring about what others have had to say, in the belief that his own training can serve to clear the ground that others have laboriously worked. But it is by no means always the case that he can distinguish the corn from the weeds, and the accumulated learning of other gardeners cannot be dismissed with the charge of empiricism (*their* empiricism against *my* theory). In any case, Derrida was not really interested in these differences I have referred to, for his thesis is that the features said to characterize speech turn out to hold for writing as well, specifically the arbitrariness and the contrasting nature of the sign. So he inverts what he sees as the accepted hierarchy and orients a theory of language not to speech but to "generalized writing." He argues that if writing is characterized by the qualities traditionally associated with it, then speech itself is a form of writing. Here he refers to the fact that graphic signs are distinguished from each other in the same way as phonemes. Reversing the hierarchy, he can now treat speech as a subspecies of writing, or rather, since the notion of writing must be broadened to include speech, we might speak, as Derrida does, of an *archi-écriture,* an archi-writing, which is the condition of both speech and writing in the narrow sense (Culler 1979: 171). So language can be seen on the model of writing as a play of differences, a proliferation of the traces and repetitions that give rise to meaning.

In this framework communicative meaning not only arises from communication but is already inscribed (hence the importance of inscription) in the structure of language. Signification always depends on differences—on the contrast, for example, between food and nonfood. Food is marked by the trace of nonfood. The signifying of events depends on differences, but these differences are themselves the products of events. This is an irresolvable dialectic, an alternation that Derrida terms *différence,* meaning "a differing" or "a deferring," a structure and a movement, active and passive.

Derrida himself is not always clear about the status of writing, for he hovers between a restricted view of the activity and an all-embracing one. "Does not pure speech require inscription—somewhat in the manner that the Leibnizian essence requires existence": That elusive pronouncement appears to suggest, following the rejection of binarism (or rather those binary distinctions he finds uncalled-for), a lack of distinction between speech and writing. Yet he follows it shortly with a sentence that suggests the opposite: "And if the necessity of becoming breath or speech restricts meaning—and our responsibility for it—writing restricts and constrains speech further still." So meaning is seen to exist independently of its formulation; it is restricted by speech just as speech is by writing. There is difference as well as similarity, but the precise form of that difference is not analyzed but simply asserted by the philosopher as deus ex machina.

Let us reconstruct rather than deconstruct that assertion. Derrida adopts an expressive view of speech: Speech does not succeed in fully expressing meaning but restricts it. An alternative position is equally plausible, that speech serves to create meaning, which can be seen as internalized speech. As for writing restricting speech, exactly the opposite could be maintained with more semblance of verisimilitude, since with writing, vocabulary, syntax, and content are widened as compared with speech, not only for cultures but usually for individuals, too. On the sentence and paragraph levels, writing complicates speech. It is difficult to imagine *Writing and Difference* in the oral mode, or rather in an oral culture. People do not speak or even think like that, they only write like that. That discrepancy may simply be an illustration of Derrida's basic problem, "that the exercise of language and thought involves us in intractable paradoxes, which we cannot escape but only repress" (Culler 1979: 156). But that is to take a very pessimistic view. Many paradoxes are not of that order but part of understanding and language itself.

The uncertainty about the distinction affects his attempt to "deconstruct" Western philosophy by linking it with the notion of the literary sign, with writing. Writing (and reading) comes to mean for the author not only the use of graphic signs in writing, in the systematic transcription of language in a visual form, but the use of other signs that may take a graphic form, not simply the mnemonic graphemes of American Indians, but even the "traces" that exist in a memory bank (an "archive") and are potentially capable of being given expression in writing in the more restricted sense. In this way reading and writing become for Derrida quasi-universal, historical activities that include, for example, reading the stars. He writes of Freud "having recourse to metaphoric models which are borrowed not from spoken language or from verbal forms, nor even from phonetic writing, but from a script which is never subject to, never exterior or posterior to, the spoken word" (Derrida 1978b: 199). This view, which I too would describe as making use of metaphor, was implicitly attacked by Lacan in his reference to hieroglyphics. To

read coffee grounds is not to read hieroglyphics. For him "natural symbolism" is not the same as the "symbolic."[1]

To equate "the writing on the wall" with writing on a blackboard is
equally unacceptable for analytical purposes since it is to fail to distinguish between graphic absence and phonemic presence, to equate a pre-
monition with an inscription. It is to make no difference between the
various signifieds of a specific signifier, and hence to take up an extreme
logocentric standpoint. The unity of the word is taken as the unity of
the object—as in punning, a verbal activity to which Derrida is singu-
larly prone and which takes phonetic similarity as the basis of substantive association; that is, playing with words (or metaphors, or analogies) as if they were "things" and hence falling into the error, at least for
some types of discourse, to which Francis Bacon long ago called attention when commenting upon the approach of earlier philosophers.[2]

Derrida also aims to criticize, or rather deconstruct, his predecessors.
Deconstructing philosophy, grammatology, is "a matter of working
through the structured genealogy of its concepts in the most scrupu-
lous fashion, from within, . . . and of determining what this history may
have concealed" (*Positions*, quoted in Culler 1979: 179). Although he
uses the terms *genealogy* and *history*, the analysis is fundamentally
ahistorical except in the limited sense of being made from within the
Western philosophical discourse that extends from Plato to Nietzsche,
Husserl, and so on. It is because of this ahistoricity that he is able to
merge writing, whose history we know and whose influence on human
culture we can assess, with speech, so that for him no differences appear between the LoDagaa or Nambikwara and the Chinese or Indians
from the standpoint of communicative action. That remains the central problem with his view of writing.

In this extended view of writing there is an aspect of intellectual fashion. In *De la grammatologie* Derrida writes: "For some time now, as a
matter of fact, here and there, by a gesture and for motives that are
profoundly necessary, whose degradation is easier to denounce than it
is to disclose their origin, one says 'language' for action, movement,
thought, reflection, consciousness, unconsciousness, experience, affec-
tivity, etc. Now we tend to say 'writing' for all that and more" (Derrida
1974: 9). The acceptance of this usage seems to me once again an irre-

sponsible attitude toward words. Then we used the term *language* as a catch-all; now we use *writing* in the same blanket fashion. Biology speaks of writing, as does cybernetics in talking of programs. Writing is connected with trace, and "in all scientific fields, notably in biology, this notion seems currently to be dominant and irreducible" (Derrida 1974: 70).

I discuss this matter of writing because the same sort of extension has been applied to the notion of archives, where once again the procedure has eroded a useful and obvious distinction. Archives are easy to pinpoint in cultures with writing. They are obviously those dusty dossiers in the cellars of *la mairie,* the tax documents accumulating in *la perception* or the treasury, the family papers stuffed higgledy-piggledy into a corner of the attic. And they are more than a collection of administrative papers recording transactions we have made. In a wider sense they are also the books we have on our shelves or in the library (especially the encyclopedias so characteristic of the Sung dynasty in China), which attempt to gather together—and in so doing to formalize—all the knowledge that we have, as well as offer critical comments on that accumulated information. That process of deconstruction leading to construction occurs partly because with writing we juxtapose different sources, older and newer, or simply different versions. It is a process that leads to an accumulation of knowledge that is significantly different from what happens in oral cultures, for it represents not simply an accumulation but a reorganization.

We can see the process of reorganization very early on in the great archives (library) of the Syrian town of Ebla, which date from the middle of the third millennium B.C.E. (c. 2400–2250 B.C.E.). Those archives include what are probably copies of original dispatches sent to officials at missions abroad or else addressed directly to other kings. "Making a copy" was an early feature of literate government, meaning that one no longer had to rely on the vagaries of oral memory. Writing things down could lead to exact, "literal" interpretations of these documents since, unlike verbal utterances, the written text can be retrieved and scanned in quite a different manner. In fact, 70 percent of the Ebla texts in the archives were administrative, another 10 percent being historical and 20 percent literary. Many of the latter were written

in Sumerian rather than the local language, for writing once again preserves the not-now-spoken; the past of language, a "dead language,"
is present in a much more concrete way.

The accumulation of documents at Ebla led to efforts to reorganize
them. There is evidence of a kind of filing system where similar documents were grouped together in baskets, producing some kind of classification, a preliminary to what we are used to in much more complex
forms in the electronic systems of the Bibliothèque nationale de France
or in the Library of Congress.

I want to insist that many of these operations are scarcely possible
without writing. In oral cultures, where I am overwhelmingly dependent upon memory store, there is clearly some kind of organizing process
at work. But the reorganizing that takes place is of a quite different
character. What I cannot do is to call up from memory a letter I wrote
to a relative some years back and read it through again. Something (a
trace?) is lodged in the memory. But that is subject not only to the process of forgetting (you can mislay a document but the contents cannot
in a concrete sense be "forgotten"), but also more especially to a process of reorganization. Maurice Halbwachs and later the British psy-
chologist Frederic Bartlett have written revealingly about this process,
what Bartlett referred to as rationalization. The oral memory, as we
know in others but do not always recognize in ourselves, may be treach-
erous and recall is selective, often influenced by individual and social
pressures. So too custodians may be, selecting among this document
and that, acting as gatekeepers of history, but the documents themselves have a material existence outside the individual of a very different kind than the memory of the spoken word; the trace is of another
order (see Steiner 1995).

Let me make the argument more substantial by giving an example
from my own experience in Africa. Myth is often seen as an archive for
oral societies, an archive that stores the accumulated knowledge of a
people, a resource that provides a key to their culture. As a result, many
have seen a myth as a completely standardized product, which each
speaker would recite with only minor variations. So, for example, we
can speak of "Zuni myth" in a quite precise way. When I first worked
on the long Bagre recitation of the LoDagaa of northern Ghana, I con-

sidered it to be archived. That is to say, I thought it was a relatively standardized utterance that people learned by heart and recited when called upon to do so, as we might learn to recite John Milton's *Paradise Lost* or some equivalent epic in French. That was how the actors usually saw the situation; all versions of the Bagre, they declared, were "one" *(boyen)*, wherever, whenever, and by whomever they were recited.

As I have remarked, in earlier days an anthropologist might have accepted this statement, since it would be all he or she could do to record a single version and there would be nothing to show the extent of variation, the "reliability" of the archive. So it might seem as if oral storage in memory and written storage in an archive produced similar results.

There were already some clues that this was not entirely the case among the LoDagaa. In the first place, there were different versions of the ritual itself, performed in different settlements. There was the "Dirt Bagre" and the "Oil Bagre" (Goody 1972: 36–37). One could accept this, as many structuralist and functionalist writers do, as a statement of the difference, even opposition, between social groups. But there is also a problem of generation. How did these differences in performance arise if transmission was perfect, word for word?

A clue to the process is given in the Bagre recitation itself. The first one I recorded, in 1950, encouraged the new entrants, the neophytes, to listen to and learn the Bagre and to sharpen their tongues "like a parrot" (Goody 1972). But at the same time it suggests that the initiates should go not only to the performances of their own lineage but to those of other groups in order to learn from them, too. In other words, it recognizes variation.

So too should I have done on theoretical grounds. The pioneering psychological work of Frederic Bartlett in *Remembering* (1932) or of Maurice Halbwachs's contributions in *Les Cadres sociaux de la mémoire* (1925) point to the transforming, rationalizing power of the oral tradition: A message begun at one point of a circle was radically changed by the time it came back to the starting point. The difference between this transmission of oral utterance and that of a written message or text is obvious. If I start at one end with a written message, it may be differently interpreted along the way but the text itself is likely to reach the end of the line as it began its journey, unless it is torn up or altered deliberately. If it is difficult to reproduce even a short oral text exactly, without taking very special measures, how much more difficult it is to transmit verbatim a very long recitation such as the Bagre. Variation is bound to creep in. Some creative inventions will appear; older elements will vanish. We may assume, in a Platonic or structuralist way, that the essence will continue, but that is far from certain, unless we conclude in a totally circular argument that what endures is bound by definition to be the essential. What would be more convincing for a scholar is if we were able to make a prediction in advance about what would be retained and what left.

As I have explained, I was able to record many further versions of this myth, and I soon realized that this conceptualization of the process was fundamentally flawed. Even the Invocation (the first dozen or so lines), which may well have been learned by heart, varied with each speaker and each recital. How much more did the full myth vary! Even basic features were not stored for posterity; succeeding generations made up new ones. The myth was in a perpetual state of transformation. So we have an infinity of oral versions of the Bagre, which in practice the actors find difficult to compare. But there are now two printed versions, which unfortunately some have begun to take as the truth, as orthodoxy, because of the prestige of writing and because they had been recited by ancestors now dead. A new measure of truth, a new concept of archive, has emerged.

From that I conclude, along with Lacan and his coffee grounds, that a written archive and oral storage are not at all the same. And on the basis of that difference we have built contemporary "civilization," in the technical sense used by prehistorians.

7
Canonization in Oral
and Literate Traditions

At the very broadest level the process of canonization is one whereby human action becomes institutionalized, authoritative, recognized as canonical. It is a highly generalized process that informs the whole of human culture, involving the creation of custom and the invention of tradition. I do not think I have anything valuable to say about how this happens; it seems to me intrinsic to the emergence of those repetitive patterns of human behavior that we refer to as culture, or in another context as the social. What I want to discuss here are two dimensions of this process, the oral and the literate (embodied in the title of this essay) and the religious and the secular.

The Religious Canon

In the standard examples of canonization, we are often dealing with written religions, so the dimensions oral/literate and religious/secular overlap. Note that I distinguish texts that are supernaturally authorized (not simply sacred in the Durkheimian sense—that would include Shakespeare) since they have some special characteristics. The written religious canon may trace its origin directly from supernatural sources or perhaps from those who were close to the supernatural. One thinks, of course, of the Ten Commandments, which represent the writings of God, and of the Torah, which is the written version of the oral tradition that accompanied this transmission. That transfer from heaven to earth was mirrored in the reception by Joseph Smith in New York State in 1827 of the tablets of gold on which were inscribed the Mormon Bible. In the case of Islam the text of the Qur'an comprises the words of Mohammad, the prophet of God. In each of these cases a written text ensures that the word of God or of his associates can be transmitted unchanged over the generations; the word is preserved in the canonical text, which is faithfully copied in a manner that encourages the art of calligraphy rather than the process of creation. Indeed, canonization forbids tampering with the text—that is left to the commentaries. Since the scribe does not invent the words, he puts his art into the form rather than the content.

A similar situation exists in the Indic religions, although the canon may be less circumscribed. The Brahmanical tradition asserts that the Vedas were *apauruṣeya*, produced by no human agency; they existed eternally and preceded the world (Goldman 1991: x). Indeed, the Vedas are even seen, logically enough, as not having an original text at all. They are supposed to be internalized by each student and transmitted orally, although they are clearly a product of writing and exist in written versions (Goody 1977a); the continuity of the canonical texts in fact depends upon having such a basis to fall back upon, as is the case with the Hebrew Bible or the Muslim Qur'an. "Other Brahmanical textual traditions trace their origins to superhuman seers or *ṛṣis* who, like the Vedic seers, had at least by implication access to similarly unconditioned texts that lend the tradition an aura of inerrancy" (Goldman 1991: x).

The canonization of written texts, however, which is what the term most frequently refers to, is in principle a deliberate process of selection: for example, whether to include or exclude the Apocrypha from the Christian canon. In principle one can analyze the procedures involved in this process, but there seems little of general relevance that one can add to particular studies.

It is clear that canonical texts of this kind have to be looked at very carefully from the historical point of view, since their preservation and transmission lie securely in the hands of the priesthood or an equivalent religious elite with whose interests they must broadly conform. That means they may give rather less attention to the interests of other groups, especially subordinate ones such as women and the lower classes, the nonelite segments of society. Both the class and gender aspects are important social facts in this context because the canon obviously stands as a religious "authority," a source of law and normative behavior for the past, present, and future, timelessly since the texts themselves are ahistorical, god-given, and enduring. What is selected may represent the interests of the selectors rather than the teaching of the Master or the interests of the whole community.

The Secular Canon

A canon of secular texts, which in Olson's definition (1994) are necessarily written (in opposition to utterances), is less circumscribed and is established by more literary and historical means, though necessarily involving the elite, the participants in high culture. For example, the Shakespearean canon, the corpus of work attributed to him, has been established over time in the first instance from the evidence of contemporaries (and by the plays being bound together) as well as by similarity of style, nowadays confirmed with the aid of a computer, which can quickly generate concordances, word counts, and so forth.

Accepting that there are principles of inclusion and exclusion in all written world religions as well as in a secular corpus of texts, I want to look at the parallel processes in oral cultures. I have initially claimed that some form of standardization is involved in all social action, but there are important differences. Let me turn first to the religious sphere.

A Canon in Oral Cultures?

I have suggested previously that religions in oral cultures are not boundary-maintaining in the same way as those of written cultures. African religions, for example, are generally eclectic, without any precise boundaries, a sum of what everybody believes rather than something fixed in a text. As a result, there are constant additions to the corpus of religious activities, some cults disappearing and new ones emerging.

With ritual and similar cultural activities, practices change quite rapidly and radically. The reasons behind these variations have to do with the generative processes that dominate that particular sphere of activity. In an early article I discussed the way that "medicine shrines" in West Africa, those connected with healing, safety, and protection against witchcraft, were continually changing (and migrating) precisely because the means adopted did not always, or even often, achieve the intended ends (Goody 1957). That is to say, to the observer there was no intrinsic "technological rationale," no necessary relationship between means and ends, so that whatever the actors perceived and practiced at one time was likely to undergo a process of disconfirmation at another. This phenomenon represented an example of the God who failed, or of a built-in obsolescence, which led not so much to a rejection of this general type of cult (though that too might take place) as to a search for a new example of what was already known. In this sphere invention was always taking place, new cults being required to replace unsuccessful ones. Nor were the results of such invention necessarily confined to the cult itself. One cult did not simply replace another like a pair of shoes. A new shrine would certainly introduce a new taboo, and that would have to be incorporated in any classificatory system that the individual utilized.

A process of this kind sheds doubt on notions that these taboos always represented fixed points in a cultural framework, since at one point in time (and for some people) such-and-such an animal or action might be forbidden and at another time (and for other people) it might not. What was out of place at one time would be in place at another. Such transitoriness is not the case with the written taboos of Leviticus, which persisted down the ages (with varying relevance for individuals) as a result of having been decontextualized in writing. I do not mean, of course, that changes in the interpretations of written taboos are not possible (though that is not what Mary Douglas was talking about [1966]). I mean only that with a written text there is a fixed point of reference to which those interpretations can return, and it is always possible for fundamentalists to revert to an earlier understanding.

Of course, there are additions and subtractions to written religions, but the scale is very different and they take place around a fixed text, which is by definition absent in oral cultures. In the latter there are no such formal boundaries, and as a consequence there is no such thing as conversion to an African religion. Asante religion is what the Asante believe in; it cannot be exported in the same way as religions with a written text. Beliefs are bound to a particular culture, so there can be no question of a shift from one set to another. One could go and live in another tribe, but there would be no possibility of converting to another religion. There is, in other words, no canon of Asante religion, since the religion is constituted by whatever everyone does. If a new cult, such as Sakrobundi, is adopted by some members of the tribe, then that is automatically part of Asante religion, at least temporarily, because there is always a turnover of cults attached to medicine shrines (see Goody 1957, 1986a). Of course, it is possible that later literates will try to resurrect an earlier oral religion, be it "witchcraft," druidical cults, or Native American religions, but these are different processes that freeze the past in reconstructing it.

Religious Change

Let me discuss first of all this problem of religious change and invention in oral cultures, because it contrasts radically with the comparative fixity of particular religions (and especially of their religious texts) in societies with writing, and it runs contrary to many established views of simple and complex societies. Scholars of all kinds, including sociologists and historians, have looked upon preliterate societies as static, stagnant, perhaps unable to change without outside intervention. That view is the one embodied in the very concept of traditional societies (as against modern or modernizing ones) not only in the thought of Max Weber but also in folk theories, and it is subject to countless transformations, in Claude Lévi-Strauss's "cold societies" (1962), in the philosopher's treatment of the Enlightenment (for example, by Jürgen Habermas and Ernst Gellner), in sociologists' analyses of the modernizing process, in Norbert Elias's "civilizing process" (1978), in Anthony Giddens's sociological modernization (1991), and in Teresa Brennan's seventeenth-century ego changes (1993). Take Giddens's characterization of modernity. "Modern institutions," he writes, "differ from all preceding forms of social order in respect of their dynamism, the degree to which they undercut traditional habits and customs, and their

global impact" (Giddens 1991: 1). That is, there is no room for canonical social forms; modernity transforms the self in a radically different
way. We may want to qualify this notion of a radical *coupure:* Has any
age not experienced the loss as well as the gain of "tradition"? What
is abundantly clear is that the rapidity of change is certainly new. But
we have to analyze this speed in the context of different subsystems,
different domains. In the domains of ritual and religion, oral cultures
are constantly changing.

Nonreligious Change

But it is not only the religious sphere of oral cultures that is subject to
such change. Spoken dialects may also experience greater pressures in
this direction than written languages (which are often "archaic," sometimes unspoken). Other aspects of culture, too, may change in similar
ways. In his work on New Guinea, Fredrik Barth has examined how
microvariations emerge in the rituals and beliefs of small neighboring
groups in the course of a generative process that involves the continuous creation of cultural elements, by exploiting the possibilities offered
by metaphor, simile, and imagery (1987). That same feature has always
struck me in Africa. Many views of such societies regard them as static,
as "cold," as unchanging. In terms of technology, slowly changing they
certainly are. Anthropologists and others also tend to see them as well
adjusted to their particular situation through decades, perhaps centuries, of quiet adaptation, and they have looked at their systems of
knowledge and classification from that same standpoint. But there is
another possible approach. In the technical sphere, continuity may be
dependent upon practices that are relatively slow to adapt to new information, which in turn inhibits the accumulation of knowledge that
would make change possible. That is understandable since, unlike
many religious practices and unlike what I am here referring to as cultural (in a loose sense), changes may need not only to be new (as with
religious cults) but also to be better in some concrete sense, more effective; that is to say, criteria of increased yield or decreased labor may
come into play.

So in technological and some other fields oral cultures are relatively static over long periods. We can see this in spatial terms by looking at adjacent peoples. In precolonial Africa, the farming systems of neighboring groups were strikingly similar; on the other hand, the magico-religious ones (rites and rituals) varied considerably. In a sense the pace of change in these two spheres is completely the opposite of what it is in written cultures. There technology (and other fields such as knowledge and education) has changed drastically over the last two thousand years, but despite increasing secularization religion has altered much less by comparison. That difference is related to the question of the canonization and the fixity of written texts. And in another way some of these considerations apply to the literary canon, which also profoundly influences the experience of many.

Standardized Utterances in Oral Cultures: The Bagre

There are, of course, some equivalents of religious *texts* in oral cultures; I refer to them as "standardized utterances." I have discussed earlier the myth of the Bagre among the LoDagaa of northern Ghana. When I first learned of this long recitation, I thought it was canonized in the sense that exact reproduction was important. I thought this for theoretical and practical reasons—theoretical, because many scholars, such as Lévi-Strauss, had treated myth as a key to culture, and as such it was a canonized product that might vary minimally in its surface structure from one recitation to the next but not in its deep structure, which was by definition homologous with the structure of other cultural domains; practical, because written accounts of oral societies give us one version of a myth or recitation, which was presumed to be a relatively fixed text. Before the advent of recording devices it was virtually impossible to get more than a single version of a long recitation, so, as with most social interaction, one had only a synchronic slice. Given then-current ideas about traditional societies, it was difficult not to think the recitation was passed down in a relatively unchanged form from generation to generation. Moreover, the actors themselves insisted that the Bagre was the "same" whenever it was performed.

Portable, lightweight tape recorders made it possible to have exact recordings of recitations in oral cultures, and at the same time, the advent of modern transport opened up the field to revisits by outside scholars. It then became very apparent that versions differed considerably over time and over place. They differed, moreover, not only in minor details but also in major (structural) features. The LoDagaa still insisted that the Bagre was one, but they were in fact referring to a notional unity of the cult.

When I looked again at my original recitation, it was not difficult to see why variations occurred despite the apparent claim of identity (Goody 1972; Goody and Gandah 1981). In the first Bagre I recorded, the new initiates are urged to go around to attend different Bagre performances and to learn what they can from them. In other words, at this level a process of incorporation is explicitly recognized. In addition, it became obvious why no one could remember exactly a long (and rather loosely structured) utterance of this kind, for there is no way of checking one's version against a fixed original; to do so by word of mouth alone is virtually impossible and anyhow not required, as the whole notion of identity, correspondence (and hence "truth," at least in one understanding), is necessarily loose in verbal (though not visual) matters. People would try to remember what they had learned (though the model too was variable), and when a Speaker could not do so exactly he would fill in, invent, develop. This was possible because what one learned was not so much a fixed utterance (as we have seen, that was virtually impossible) as a way of reciting, of composing recitativo, of fitting speech into a relatively standard rhythmic frame. Indeed, a good reciter was one who had mastered this technique and who could elaborate an incident in the course of his recitation without much hesitation.

I have discussed earlier the extent of the variations in versions collected within the radius of about a mile over some twenty years. Going further afield, one finds much wider variations. There is no evidence of a fixed utterance existing over long periods of time, as we see with written religious texts. In other words, canonization is virtually impossible, even if beliefs and action as well as recitation look fixed at a particular moment in time. It was one of the problems of functional and structural analyses, which had many advantages, that they did not sufficiently allow for this possibility.

The Contrast between Religious
Texts and Religious Utterances

Let us look at the consequences of this contrast between religious text and religious utterance. If we carry out excavations in South Asia, Southeast Asia, or Europe for the period about a thousand years back, we come across three-dimensional sculptural forms that we can place in a specific mythological or theological tradition: in Europe the crucifix or the reliquary statue, in South Asia forms that we can readily identify as Siva or Ganesh. Of course, we possess literary texts that may help explain the finds; more significant is that these icons exist today and part of their meaning (but clearly not their whole context) can be projected backward. Nor is it only a question of time, for similar finds (with regional variations) occur over a wide geographic area stretching in the Christian case from the Sinai Desert to the Irish Sea. I do not wish to overstress the resemblances across cultures, but one gains major clues to the interpretation of such objects by reading the text, even though that has been continuously reinterpreted. Nevertheless, it has remained basically a fixed text (qua text, not its readings and interpretation) from the time of the Dead Sea Scrolls virtually to the present day. That fixity is a matter of inspection, not of dispute. It is the same in India. I do not refer to the unlikely story of the Rig Veda having been transmitted unaltered in oral form for over a thousand years, but to the existence of much earlier texts that embody relevant aspects of the mythology.

I want to draw a limited contrast of that situation with Africa, where an archaeological dig will produce some objects whose technological use, if not whose entire meaning, we know or can deduce, that is, hoe blades, axe heads, and scrapers, and other objects about which nothing can be inferred and which are often called "ritual objects," or in some cases "ancestral figures." That is true of the stone sculptures of Sierra Leone or the array of clay figurines from northern Ghana, some with querulous faces, that have been assigned to the "Koma." Of these objects we know virtually nothing of their use or meaning.

This difference has to do with the power of writing to establish and validate a continuing set of beliefs in a canonized form that persists over time. That textual continuity represents power, especially in the hands of religious specialists, and therefore encourages a particularly conservative use of literacy skills. Since the teaching of writing—which itself may have been invented in the course of mercantile activity, as Schmandt-Bessarat's work suggests for Mesopotamia—was virtually everywhere (except China) taken over by the priesthood, which has shown a strong attachment to canonized texts for which it is the intermediary, thus bolstering its position, instruction often took on forms that supported and even froze the status quo. But as I have remarked, we have to look at the impact of the text sectorally, and indeed contextually. Obviously not all written texts embody knowledge that is fixed over time, not always in literature (although we have our classics, we can add to their range) nor at all in science (except over the short term). In literature, new authors (for, with writing, works are more readily attributed to individuals, like the signed work of art) constantly produce new products, especially with the increased circulation following the advent of printing, the increase in demand through education (hence in audience), and supply pressures from the booksellers. In science, in the broad sense of knowledge of the physical world, one of the great potentialities of writing was that one could readily build upon earlier texts in a cumulative manner, so that last year's textbook becomes this year's reject. That is the opposite of canonization. Yet not everything works in the same direction, because even scientific uses of writing involve the canonization of cognitive instruments such as arithmetic tables, which, at least before the advent of the pocket calculator, pupils had to learn by heart, to internalize, in order to proceed to more complex calculations. Much earlier knowledge becomes canonical in relatively arbitrary ways, for example, the division of plants and animals into species and families. The supreme example of this process is the alphabet itself, the basis of our writing system. We learn this system of representing sounds in the purely arbitrary order of ABC, which has existed since 1500 B.C.E.; it gives us enormous power to organize, retrieve, and recall information when that information is alphabetized in the form of a directory, index, or telephone book.

Gender and Canon

We also have to look at the situation contextually from another stand-point, gender, which is an important factor in the composition, forma-tion, and maintenance of a canon. Literacy put great power in the hands of the priesthood, almost entirely male, as well as of the (often exclusively male) elite whom they taught. That represented power vested in the minority of the literate over the majority of the illiterate (dis-proportionately female), who had only indirect access to the canonized text. With certain exceptions this situation persisted in the religious domain for nearly five thousand years, from the invention of scripts through the post-Renaissance spread of schools and down to the nine-teenth century, when universal education began to become a reality in some of the major powers of the world.

Earlier on, formal education was virtually limited to males, partly because of the restrictions of the priesthood. Women were largely ex-cluded from classical education, as they are from the second stage of the Bagre rites and indeed in principle from the knowledge held by many secret societies. However, a recent anthology of Indian women writers traces their participation back to the sixth century B.C.E., to the very beginning of alphabetic writing in the subcontinent. A similar anthol-ogy could be constructed for Europe, running from Sappho through women religious writers to the female troubadours and on to the nov-elists and dramatists of the late seventeenth century. The past inequal-ities between men and women in matters of literacy are well known; formal schooling of an advanced kind was provided primarily if not exclusively for males. Yet there were ways in which women did acquire the ability to read and write, often through the family, so that they were not totally excluded from these processes of cultural participation and creation, especially in the secular domains (there are other processes in which they dominated, as Gordon Childe pointed out for the more practical spheres [1942]), in the way that they are excluded from par-ticipating in the recitation (and hence production) of the LoDagaa myth of the Bagre, specifically from the second phase of initiation and hence of the "deeper" myths (see Goody 1972; Goody and Gandah 1981). One can more readily exclude them from public occasions in an oral culture, which is when the religious recitations occur. It is less easy to keep the Bible or the Bhagavad-Gita out of their hands. Partly that is a result of general spiritual equity, a feeling that women cannot be denied salvation; this was of particular importance in societies with "diverging devolution" (in post–Bronze Age societies parental property devolves through both sexes), where the greater longevity of women means that much property ends up in their hands and their salvation is therefore of considerable importance to religious entrepreneurs (Goody 1983). It is also partly because in conjugal families, there is not always a male to be instructed, and so a woman is substituted; even when sons are present, there is sometimes a tendency for young siblings to be treated in a relatively equitable manner whatever the sex, just because they are from the same mother and father.

Writing and Anticanonization

The hegemonic force of the canon or of the dominant ideology does not go entirely unchallenged in the written word. Its power is not always wielded by nor confined to those in authority who hold political office. Writing can also be used for countercultural, revolutionary, or critical purposes; that development is more characteristic of printing than of manuscript cultures, since it is the masses that have to be organized, a process that is facilitated by the mass production and brisker circulation of texts. We must also see the initial spread of some literate religions, especially Christianity, as related to the power of the text, first written, then printed.

Conclusions

The process of canonization, as I understand it, derives from the nature of the written text, which encourages boundary-maintaining religions with an approved corpus of holy works. While in oral societies religious utterances such as myths may appear to the actors to be canonized, the process of transmission is in fact much less constraining. Canonical written texts are copied; oral myths are re-created in repetition. Of course, there is also a process of secular canonization in both written and oral cultures. Literature falls into this category, as do some aspects of scientific endeavor, but much new written activity encourages the criticizing and complementing of the old, including the classics. In oral cultures there is less deliberate search for change, but as with myth, change is constantly taking place, even if the actors at any particular moment view culture as canonical. That is the paradox of formation and transmission: One can have a fixed text only with the aid of a medium that in other contexts invites decanonization.

8

Technologies of the Intellect: Writing and the Written Word

Many of those who write about the history of mankind consider the emergence of the species as linked to the advent of material technology, the ability to make things, the arrival of Homo faber, man the tool maker. Whatever boundary cases exist, that is clearly an area in which a quantum shift took place, cumulative change leading to rapid advance.

Others stress the emergence of man as a language-using animal, though it is difficult to reconstruct when this phase began. The technical differences between the systems of oral communication of men and other animals is a yet more complicated boundary, one that has been subtly dealt with by Charles Hocket (1960). While systems of verbal communication display a series of morphological differences, a quantum jump clearly exists when we come to language itself. While this leap forward does not concern material objects—things, in the usual sense of the word—I want to suggest that it does fall within the realm of technology as defined in the words of the National Academy of Sciences, quoted by Robert McCormick Adams (1996), namely, "codified ways of deliberately manipulating the environment to achieve some material objective." What we are dealing with are changes in modes of communication rather than in modes of production.

I need to interpolate an additional comment on the concept of technology because it is often used in a very limited way. For example, if I claim that the technology of hoe agriculture in Africa has limited certain developments in, say, the growing of cereals, I am not characterizing a situation that can be changed by parachuting in a crate of plows, for involved in the shift is the whole social organization of production and of use. To put the matter at its simplest, the use of this technology means training bullocks and altering attitudes toward livestock. Production means forges, carpentry, village specializations. Change involves land tenure as well as land use; it affects the division of labor, household organization, and more.

Especially when I speak of writing as a technology of the intellect, I refer not just to pen and paper, stylus and tablet, as complex as these instruments are, but to the training required, the acquisition of new motor skills, and the different uses of eyesight, as well as to the products themselves, the books that are stacked on the library shelves, objects that one consults and from which one learns, and which one may also, in time, compose.

Changes in modes of communication are internal to the individual as well as external to him. Language is the prototypical social fact in the Durkheimian sense; it is both of society, like the wheel, and internalized during our upbringing. That has been the case over a long period of time, so the presence of language may even have altered our physiological makeup by leading to the enlargement of the right hemisphere of the brain.

Just as language has altered our ability to deal with the world at the level of cognition, of understanding, of manipulation, the same is true of the next great step in the development of modes of communication, that is, of writing, which occurred some five thousand years ago in the Near East. While anthropologists and linguists concerned with the human revolution have given much attention to the role of language, and while prehistorians interested in later revolutions looked at the Bronze Age from the standpoint of introducing the culture of cities based on intensive agriculture, too little attention has been paid to the implications of the invention of writing, which is often treated simply as a device for recording and processing language. It is much more, but it clearly has different kinds of effect on mankind than language itself does, for while speech is a universal attribute of human beings—a defining attribute, many would argue, at least of *Homo sapiens*—writing has characterized only some societies and only a proportion of human beings in them.

Until some hundred years ago, even in societies with writing, a majority of members did not know how to read and write. Written cultures were minority cultures. Again, the time depth was of a different scale, language having been a human attribute of "civilized" society for perhaps twenty times as long as writing.

It was those very societies where only a limited proportion could read and write that made such fundamental contributions to the development of knowledge. While universal literacy was rarely an issue until the nineteenth century, while the capacity to read and write was a minority phenomenon from one point of view, the long-term presence of these activities profoundly affected the internal and external lives of the whole of the population. In sixteenth-century London, the groundlings formed part of the audience of the Elizabethan theater, essentially a literary theater. A Religion of the Book dominated their lives and thoughts on other occasions, through sermons, buildings, stained glass, and paintings, and in countless other ways. The political system was organized through written decrees and public records. The economy, as it expanded, made increasing use of more complex accounting procedures, of manuals of practice, and of knowledge accumulated in writing. In all these ways writing intertwined with the lives of the inhabitants, cognitively as well as organizationally.

That situation has changed rapidly over the last century, during which universal literacy has become a central aim of Western countries. More recently the same aim has been adopted by societies that a hundred years ago were virtually untouched by the written word. European colonization from the fifteenth century on had ensured that nearly all societies not only came into contact with writing but adopted it for external and internal purposes. Earlier colonizations, of Greece, Rome, Assyria, India, and China, had similar results in other parts of the world where the teaching of writing and the creation of literates were seen as a fundamental part of the "civilizing" mission of colonial and imperial rule. Today that mission has taken on a universal aspect for individuals as well as societies. It would be impossible to imagine a purely oral society as a member of the United Nations, or indeed a purely oral tribal population within a national state.

It is because of the largely cumulative interaction of apparently external and internal elements that I have spoken of "technologies of the intellect" in the context of writing and its products. Technology has had a bad press from scholars. Scientists look down on it; humanists look away from it. We disguise its products under other heads, so that, as at the Smithsonian Institution in Washington, D.C., the National Museum of History and Technology becomes the National Museum of American History. But the public still looks up to it as a way, by and large, of improving the quality of life, or at the very least the standard of living. *Technology* is a broad, comprehensive term that covers a field overlapping with scientific knowledge. Like science, many of its branches have a generally cumulative development. Particular techniques often proceed stepwise, largely but not entirely in a direction of greater efficiency (in terms of a calculus of means and ends). Of course, the ends vary, as do the means. Nevertheless, a progression is reasonably clear for a number of areas of human activity, even though there are times of stasis, blind alleys, and occasionally the decay of useful arts of which Rivers wrote. One has only to think of the production of cloth or of the development of transport. No one would suggest a process of universal improvement; in techniques, perhaps, but not in qualities or standards. Some of the changes provide alternative courses of action, while others may involve a step backward, but the general trend is difficult to refute. Even if some sects, some romantics, some Luddites, some critical intelligences express their doubts, they rarely give up the advantages of the telephone or the motor car. Social pressures are indubitably involved; if the majority accepts certain technologies, the rest are pushed to follow. But given constant ends, we can talk of improved means. These changes (improvements) often take the form of entailed change, that is to say, one invention in machines for spinning or weaving builds upon a previous one; the changes themselves are incremental.

One of the aspects of technology that makes some humanists bristle is the assumption of external determinacy by nonhuman forces. There are three errors involved in this contention. Any determinacy (single-factor causation) relates to the sequential entailment of improvements, which tend increasingly to be supracultural, extending beyond particular cultures. Other particular cultural factors influence rates of invention (improvement), processes of adoption and adaptation, and so forth. The problem here is always one of sorting out the more general and the more specific; to call vaguely upon culture is the antithesis of analysis. Because of the nature (in general) of the means-ends relationships in technology, there is inevitably a degree of autonomy from other (socio-cultural) factors. Each society, each group, each individual adapts the bicycle to his own context, but only within limits. Some of the social implications remain constant.

Second, in no sense is technology nonhuman, since it is developed and used by human minds and hands. Finally, the products of technology are external only in a formal sense, since they are formed by humanity and in turn form humanity. A loom or a sword is no more external than a book, although the technology of the intellect of which the latter is a product involves a special kind of interaction between the human being and his environment. Of course, this is true to some extent of all technology that influences us and our actions internally in a variety of ways. With a pen in our hands, we are different than when we carry a sword or work on the loom; we have different roles that structure our perceptions. But writing has a particular kind of internal influence since it changes not only the way we communicate but the nature of what we communicate, whether to others or to ourselves. I do not mean only that writing and reading provide special ways of reflection; it is difficult for many of us to imagine how we would operate without the kind of visual interaction with the word that they render possible, the kind that is involved in making a flow chart or entering items in a list (which in certain contexts may act as a flow chart). Not all intellectual tasks require the intervention of such techniques, of course. Instruments of many kinds are available in societies without writing. But they remain at a level that does not permit the organization of the more complex tasks concerned with the development and accumulation of knowledge. In this endeavor we are aided by "tools." To some scholars, tools are things used by other people, gardeners or mechanics. On the contrary, the use of the hands—and the eyes—is intrinsic to intellectual work. The minute coordination of movements of the eye and hand is crucial to brushwork in Chinese painting and calligraphy, just as it is to the use of chopsticks; one of the problems about extending education in writing and reading in eighteenth-century France was precisely that peasants were not accustomed to the necessary movements of the eye and the control of the fingers. The tools of literates provide their societies with technologies of a cognitive kind, technologies that are themselves tools, for tools create further tools.

The material/immaterial dichotomy, dear to so many, is irrelevant here. The difference between writing and speech is sometimes phrased in terms of writing providing a material counterpart of thought, in contradistinction to speech—hence its ability to persist through time and space, independent of the human actor (except, of course, for the writer himself). While the characterization is mainly correct, the critical distinction is not between material and immaterial but between visual (or rather visual on a relatively enduring medium: clay, stone, palm leaf, paper) and nonvisual. However, the existence of a visual component means that there is always a design element, a spatial element, with the written word. The Chinese letters hanging on the wall are a picture as well as a saying, with a close connection to painting itself.

What writing permits is the mixture of graphic modes especially important as announcements or advertisements. In the ancient world, and particularly in ancient Rome, much use was made of writing at a municipal level. One can also view the engraving of codes, such as the Cretan Code of Gortyn or the yet earlier Code of Hammurabi, as making an announcement to the citizens. In the case of Hammurabi, the announcement took the form of sculpture on which the text was engraved. That is typical of much early graphic art, such as Egyptian tomb paintings. The mixture is also typical of later advertisements, especially if one includes the logo as well as the statements, the coat of arms as well as the motto.

Many anthropologists are reluctant to see these techniques as facilitating cognitive advances, as instruments of intellectual operation. Their immersion in "other cultures" has led them to be suspicious of many of the lines drawn between these cultures and our own. This is rightly so from some standpoints, but wrongly so from others. One cannot overlook the advances in knowledge that have been made by mankind; that would be to engage in a sentimental relativism that neglects the welcome given to most of these techniques, or their products, by the vast majority of people when offered the opportunity. That includes the book as well as the sword or the loom.

How does the notion of technology apply to systems of writing? Looking at the first level, that of technique, we know little about the events leading up to the invention of logographic scripts, especially in the Egyptian, Chinese, and Mayan instances. However, in the Mesopotamian case, Schmandt-Bessarat has worked out a sequence, not undisputed, by which commercial tokens developed into a full writing system capable of representing the whole range of speech forms (1992).

Historically, logographic scripts were followed by ones based on phonetic units or syllables, and later by the invention of the alphabet. The sequence of events is more complex and the advantages of the later systems less unambiguous than we thought some years ago in the days when European scholars such as Eric Havelock drew attention to the critical value of the alphabet for the ancient Greeks. Once you accept the aim of universal literacy, then the advantages of adopting a syllabic or alphabetic script become greater because such scripts are simpler to learn. The alphabet is a more abstract calculus representing not words, as in a logographic script, but phonemes, which do not themselves carry semantic meaning.

With a vastly reduced number of components, it becomes initially more difficult but in the end easier to learn. Logographs, such as Chinese characters, can be learned one by one. Everyone, even without schooling and language learning, can be partially literate. In Japan I have only to recognize the sign, not the word, for *entrance* or *men* to be able to use the parking lot or the toilet; I do not have to understand a whole system, as with the alphabet.

The problem of recognition involves differences in degree, but the extent to which alphabetic and logographic scripts differ is clear when, as an ignoramus, you try to decipher street names, bus destinations, or train stations in Arabic as opposed to Chinese. On the other hand, earlier access to certain logographs means that mastery of the corpus tends to come later. In East Asia a knowledge of perhaps six thousand characters is required for entrance to a university, a quantity that is sufficient to daunt many a potential scholar, leaving less learning time for substantive subjects or drastically lengthening the student's working day, as with the 40 percent of Japanese children who attend *juku,* evening school, after they have finished with the normal day.

If there are technical advantages to the alphabet, why do others hang on to their own more cumbersome systems? The first reason must be that only with the retention of the script (and language) can one continue to have access to all those cumulative records, to the classical literature, to the bodies of knowledge built up by one's predecessors— the very things that writing has made possible. It is true that one can translate and transcribe, but the cost is heavy and, as with the rendering of Chaucer into modern English, something is always felt to be lost. Second, logographic scripts have their own advantages. Being largely nonphonetic, the same sign can represent words in different dialects, different languages, much as the figure 1 represents the same number throughout the world, whether it is *one, uno, eins,* or *boyen.* Written communication is possible between the speakers of a variety of tongues, rather the way Latin served as a lingua franca in medieval Europe.

This discussion of comparative advantage has been dominated by the Western humanist tradition that placed so much emphasis on the achievement of the Greeks, their own spiritual ancestors. But it is important to realize that the shift to the alphabet is not so crucial to many kinds of social and intellectual development as was once thought. Certainly in Greece writing became more widely available than before and penetrated many areas of human life, giving rise to new genres of writing and knowledge. That development was partly an effect of adapting the Semitic alphabet. I say adapting because it is clear that the Greek adaptation of the Phoenician script was a significant but relatively small step in the establishment of a complete phonetically based system. Vowels apart, the alphabet emerged some 750 years before the Greeks, in around 1500 B.C.E., where it was used for composing the Torah and the Old Testament as well as the New Testament before spreading eastward in the form of Aramaic and Arabic and giving rise to scripts as far afield as Tagalog in the Philippines. And well before that a degree of phonetic transcription was part and parcel of all known logographic scripts.

Furthermore, much of what has been attributed to the Greeks existed embryonically in earlier written civilizations. Some was embedded in Egyptian and Mesopotamian antecedents. Equally much was achieved by societies in East Asia that retained their logographic script. The image of a static Oriental society beloved by many social scientists has to be discarded. In a volume of *Science and Civilisation in China* (1986), Joseph Needham compares botanical knowledge in the East and West, concluding that at the time of Theophrastus's great work, Chinese botanical knowledge had attained roughly the same level. And that was not a matter of the local folk systems, but of the accumulation and analysis of knowledge in written form. There are countless similar examples to do with the advancement of knowledge. Earlier discussions now seem very ethnocentric, Eurocentric, or Near East–centered, especially when we look at the current achievements not only of Japan but of Taiwan, Korea, and Hong Kong, committed as they are to the use of scripts of the logographic kind. Much of what has been attributed to Greece was possible with other writing systems, and some of those possibilities were achieved. Undoubtedly the overemphasis on Greek achievement in the alphabet and elsewhere was partly due to the ethnocentric insistence on the achievements of the Aryan-speaking peoples. Like many other European assumptions, these notions need to be drastically reviewed in the light of recent events, but modified, not rejected in favor of a diffuse culturalism that explains everything and nothing. It has long been clear to me, and has become increasingly clearer, that such arguments underplay the significance of writing in general at the expense of promoting particular forms of script, and it is on the general implications of writing that I want to concentrate, if only because it is obvious that whatever learning problems the Chinese script and the mixed scripts of Japan impose upon new entrants, those forms of writing have made possible many advances, including not only the adaptation to industrial capitalism but also its development.

In his account of the growth of the use of writing in Britain in the Middle Ages, M. T. Clanchy (1979) has a chapter entitled "The Technology of Writing," in which he discusses the nature of the instruments and the scripts that were employed. When I originally spoke of writing as a technology of the intellect, I was not thinking primarily of the immediate implications of different types of script, the level of technique, but rather of what kinds of cognitive or intellectual operations could be carried out in writing that were impossible, difficult, or less efficient in speech. Some of these are obvious and derive directly from the durability of the materials used for written language. We can read, and substantially understand, the contents of a letter written on a Sumerian clay tablet, whereas the oral conversations of nonliterate contemporaries have disappeared without trace. Those records, and their analysis, can lead to a changed understanding of the past, which in turn affects the present and the future. Leaving aside the implications for history, it permits the accumulation of knowledge in a way that is inconceivable in a society where virtually everything has to be stored in the human memory. According to Daniel Boorstin, a former librarian of Congress, "While knowledge is steady and cumulative, information is random and miscellaneous." Knowledge is a matter of understanding and interpretation, too, but one has to have stored information in the first place.

The implications are not simply quantitative, although we may be tempted to think so when we look around at the proliferating contents of museums and libraries. Of greater significance is what one can do with the information so recorded and stored. With writing one can reorganize it, just as one can by making a list of the items that one wishes to buy or of the things one has to do, subsequently reordering them in a more helpful, "logical" way, in terms of urgency, accessibility, or whatever other criterion is appropriate.

But the extent of the feedback on behavior is much more extensive than these examples imply, especially in the fields associated with the accumulation and development of various forms of knowledge. Let me look very briefly at the very simple procedures of social anthropology as an example of a not very systematic knowledge system. We speak of anthropology as an observational inquiry directed to the study of human interaction. But the critical feature is not so much the making as the recording of the observations, not so much what we choose to notice as what we choose to record, because subsequent work is largely based on field notes, and others will base their knowledge of a people on what we have written down, with the help of our bibliography, being unable to repeat what we have done in any precise way. For recording, the traditional instrument is the notebook, which has more recently been supplemented by the tape recorder and cameras (still, motion picture, and video). But tape recordings of speech are of little use until they are themselves transcribed and translated, that is, put into writing. In the same way, visual material is of minimal use until a way has been found to code—that is, put into writing—the activities they record.

In presenting the results of one's research, it is to the field notes that one returns over time, and the longer the time, the more dependent one is on them, preferring to accept their version of events rather than that of memory alone. While there may be a variety of ways of presenting this material, especially for the general public, the major contributions to an ongoing field of knowledge are made in written form, such as papers, memos, and monographs. Only in this way can those results be studied by students eager to fill out the oral presentation, as well as by all those scattered around the globe who want to subject one's discussion to critical examination, reviewing the text and suggesting an alternative or variant reading.

Consider what I can do with the written that I cannot do with the oral. I am not confined to the face-to-face situation. I can examine the work of, say, Lévi-Strauss, at a distance; I can reconsider it from the standpoint of its internal logic, the sequencing of ideas, and I can set empirical statements about the Kwakiutl against those of other observers such as Helen Codere, looking for the confirmations and the contradictions. To translate those operations into a more experimental context, I can comment upon the argument and I can observe the discrepancies in empirical findings, either of which may lead me to propose a new resolution or undertake a critical experiment.

I have deliberately referred to the perception of logical relations and contradiction because these were the very features that the French philosopher Lucien Lévy-Bruhl seized upon to distinguish the thinking or mentalities of advanced from primitive societies or, better, complex from simple ones (1910). His ideas have been widely rejected, often in favor of a diffuse relativism that sees all human mental processes as being homologous, if not identical. So, of course, they largely are at the level of genetically inherited ability, since, unlike language, later changes in modes of communication have left no permanent imprint on the human brain. But where this anthropological relativism loses its way and therefore opens the door to the very ethnocentric interpretations it finds so reprehensible is that it fails to recognize the interaction between technologies, either material or of the intellect, and human minds, and hence overlooks the capacities of those human beings to do different things with words, with information, with communication itself. To put it another way, such capacities are attributed to "culture," meaning a random difference between cultures rather than the roughly sequential development of forms of human culture.

If we look at the question of "logic" and "contradiction" in relation to modes of communication, we find that all human beings have the ability to perform (so-called) logical operations and observe contradictions. But their capacity to do so varies, not simply randomly by "cultures" but in a relatively systematic way. These processes are potentially enhanced when one can review someone's written argument, as distinct from his speech. For example, one can then examine more or less simultaneously the beginning and the end, what he says he is going to do and what he actually does do in the conclusion, as well as the steps by which the argument has proceeded. Hence the emphasis on that Aristotelian injunction, applied to essays, papers, and theses as well as to theatrical productions, that written forms should have a beginning, a middle, and an end, not simply in a generalized van Gennepian way, but much more precisely, so we can see whether the end ties up with the beginning, logically and without contradiction. There are more formal ways in which logic, of the syllogistic kind, and contradiction, as laid out by Aristotle, are characteristic of written rather than oral cultures. That does not mean that oral societies cannot perceive contradiction and do not have forms of sequential reasoning, but they do not have the kinds of techniques for carrying out these operations that literacy permits or encourages.

I have described this process as one of making the implicit explicit. At one level that is true, for all languages have a grammar. But "grammars" occur only in societies with writing. However, the matter does not stop with explicitness. Because the "grammar" organizes, it reorganizes the linguistic material and changes the actual situation not merely in an academic sense, not only by making the study of language more "scientific," but by a process of feedback whereby the "grammar" becomes a model for speakers of that natural language, and hence may delay change or institutionalize usage (as with the initial *h* in eighteenth-century England).

The same is true of dictionaries. Words everywhere have meanings. But dictionaries do not only teach how to spell; they spell out meanings in a standardized way, "dictionary definitions," which then become the norm and the starting point of a discussion. How often do academic discussions begin with something like "The *OED* [or *Webster's*] defines X as . . ."?

So when I use the phrase "technology of the intellect" about writing, I am thinking mainly not about the primary level of physical instrumentation but about the way that writing affects cognitive or intellectual operations, which I take in a wide sense as relating to the understanding of the world in which we live, especially the general methods we use for this. Let us move to the secondary level of information and knowledge. In the first instance we are dealing with storage. In oral cultures this storage is virtually limited to the human memory. What is not held in memory, that is, not learned in face-to-face or directly experienced situations, literally ceases to be, ceases to exist. One cannot retrieve something that leaves no memory trace, a fact that profoundly impressed me in longitudinal studies of the recitation of the LoDagaa myth of the Bagre, which I carried out for more than twenty-five years.

In societies with a written corpus, the position is very different. In the first place, the potential exists to store an infinity of information in a more or less permanent form—not, of course, at the level of the individual but at the level of the archive, the library, and now the computer, all of which hold information in graphic form.

In order to acquire or manipulate this information, to think about it, the individual has to know how to retrieve it. That is what much education is about: learning to read, later learning to use encyclopedias, dictionaries, reference books, and textbooks in which knowledge in a particular field has been described and assessed, as in the *Summa Theologica* of Thomas Aquinas. One can also acquire this knowledge in a mediated way, which is again what much of education is about. Students may be led to the latest developments in a field by a teacher who presents them with the results of his reading. In theory and sometimes in practice, the achievements of what is essentially a written activity can be passed on to those who have no knowledge of reading and writing. They may be taught how to look for the latest quark, but their subsequent contributions will inevitably be limited, or seized upon by those who control the written word, since the field ultimately depends upon the use of graphic procedures, of which writing is the most crucial.

The first level of technology we have been considering is the script and the writing materials themselves. The second is the level of storage and its implications. But it is the third that to my mind is the most interesting as well as the most important. It is also the most difficult to handle. At the first level, each kind of instrument used and each type of script developed has different implications for communication and for social life more generally. The hard-baked clay tablets of Mesopotamia provided better long-term recall than less durable substances used elsewhere; paper (papyrus) preserves well in the desiccated environment of Egypt, less well in the damper climes across the Mediterranean. Scripts have obvious differences, the implications of which we have already discussed.

The second level has to do with the material products of these scripts themselves, the immense quantities of books stored in libraries and archives from the days of Ebla over the next forty-five hundred years, and the immense quantities of information contained in those books, ranging from gazetteers, atlases, and phone directories to treatises on botany and nuclear physics and through to poetry, drama, and literature in general. Societies without writing lack storage facilities of this kind and scale, and hence lack some of the essential instruments for retrieval, for cumulative knowledge, and for a new type of cultural tradition, not to speak of new forms of knowledge and new artistic genres, such as the novel, the sonnet, or even, as I have suggested, the epic.

The third level of tools is the product of the interaction between the human mind and the written word, which is external to the actor in a way spoken language is not. Once again the difference is a matter of degree, but with writing the modus operandi of the human intellect is changed by this internal-external interaction. These tools are not "material" in the same sense as the first two. Some of their features I have discussed elsewhere, but never with any attempt to be inclusive, nor am

I even sure how one would obtain closure or whether what we have isolated would display any homogeneity as "cognitive procedures." While I cannot examine these in any detail, I want to list very simply some of the devices. The first of these is listing itself, which was such a common feature of early writing that scholars spoke of *Listenwissenschaft* as a separate branch of Mesopotamian activity (Goody 1977a: 80). The making of those lists involves taking words, usually with connected meanings, out of the flow of speech and considering them as things in themselves. While there is nothing in principle to stop this from happening in oral societies, it rarely occurs. On the other hand, the establishment of bounded semantic categories, often indicated by a particular sign in logographic scripts, is a characteristic of written language, and one that places systems of classification and categorization on a different footing than is usual with the folk systems of oral societies, where the categories have to be elicited and cannot usually just be read off. The lists comprise a much wider range than category lists, and include shopping lists, nominal rolls, and administrative records of all sorts, which display a distinctly nonspeechlike structure. They lead directly to tables, which are essential devices for much analytic discourse of a written kind and are impossible to conceive without writing; again, they provide a different set of dimensions for the process of reading off analogies and polarities, columns and rows. Such tables have the effect of forcing thought into binary forms, even when these may not be appropriate; arrange three items in double-column tables and the search is on for the fourth term, for the top quark or the missing element in a Parsonian four-square table. Such procedures may be generative, as was the case with the atomic table. Equally they may lead down blind alleys, as often seems to be the case with the sociological or anthropological equivalents. The use of these devices does not inevitably lead to cumulative knowledge, but they are intrinsic to its development.

Mathematical tables constitute such a technology of the intellect for which writing was a prerequisite. They are completely parallel to the electronic calculator. Indeed, they are entailed in a series of technological shifts, of a partly unilinear kind, that involves the abacus, the slide rule, and the calculator. In this sense they form a set not unlike the technologies in the cotton industry. They can be seen as "entailed" by the increasing rationality or efficiency of the means-ends relationship (with both means and ends being variables).

Take another table, the square of magic numbers. Can this be described in the same way? It is made possible by writing, and the actors may see it as equally instrumental, though for what we would call magical or religious reasons. It assists them in their understanding of the world. To some extent it can be seen as entailed in a set of techniques such as the crossword puzzle, a game as distinct from magic, but again one that may be linked to the development of problem-solving capacities.

The differences are shaded, involving the judgment of the observer. Entailment necessarily does. One can see entailment only when, for example, one technique supersedes another for rational reasons (for instance, greater productivity, not simply because one wants a change). Moreover, the degree of entailment varies. Second, one is making a judgment in terms of the rationality of the ends as well as of the means. These observer judgments may be of limited value, but we have to make them and it is quite legitimate to do so. We have to allow for "developments" that do not develop, for "improvements" that do not improve. But we do so with all changes, whether of the intellect or not, and it seems logical to look at both types of table as part of the same set.

I have already referred to the formalization involved in "logic" as well as the processes of reorganizing information and reviewing an argument. Each is significantly altered by the introduction of writing, including the ordering of information under numeric and alphabetic heads. So too the processes of labeling and the giving of instructions take on different dimensions, just as space does with the development of mapping and time with that of clocks, both of them devices involving graphic though not directly literate measurements. Most significant, perhaps, is the development of methods of proof, which Geoffrey Lloyd has analyzed in his work on Greek science (1979); while the social ambience in Greece was relevant to the emergence of these methods, we find similar procedures of a less advanced kind in Mesopotamia, as Jean Bottéro has pointed out (1977). The Euclidian geometry that was still being taught in schools when I grew up, with its concluding abbreviation QED, *quod erat demonstrandum*—not to speak of the whole notion of algebra, with its substitution of abstract letters for concrete numbers, or forms of symbolic logic, where letters stand for words or sentences—seems very dependent upon writing.

I could go on listing such devices in a not very systematic manner, but one last point will suffice. In a discussion of an issue so fundamental for education, learning, and research (and of much else besides), namely, that of questions, the point has been made that in preindustrial societies the nature of social relationships makes it difficult to separate the information function of questions from the command function (E. Goody 1978). Here again writing seems a relevant variable since it involves a process of reflexivity, of bouncing thoughts between oneself and a piece of paper, which makes it easier to effect this separation and to ask questions, especially open-ended questions, even of oneself: Why am I here (on the philosophical level), why does the world go round (on the empirical, scientific level)? It is the nature of this interaction—activity-specific, incremental in many ways, but highly significant—that makes it difficult for differences between literate and nonliterate performance to be picked up by the usual form of psychological test alone. The differences lie at the level of interaction between the self and an object, the written word, be it my word or someone else's.

When one regards the processes of writing and reading as interactive—me, within, interacting with what is without, either your words or my words on a piece of paper—then the boundaries between the internal and the external, the material and the immaterial, dissolve or need to be reformulated. But as I have earlier remarked, the total effects of writing are not only interactive in this immediate sense. Some are; the reformulation of information and the use of maps are procedures that demand literacy as well as writing. Others do not make such demands, though they may perhaps be considered to do so over the longer term. The example to which I turn again (and there are many possibilities) is the mathematical table. That is essentially the product of writing, but one that can be taught to and learned by those who can neither read nor write. Yet it provides those who use it with a special cognitive tool, a technology of the intellect.

Nevertheless, most of the subsequent advances in knowledge are carried out by those who can read and write, rather than those who cannot. That raises the question of whether thinking when writing is different from thinking when speaking (or even when one is silent). Silent thinking is still basically linguistic thinking, and one can take one's time with it. There is, however, always the problem of collecting one's thoughts, as the phrase goes—rather as if thoughts were the fluffy, wind-blown seeds of the dandelion and one had to pluck them out of the air. And one does, too, for they are apparently immaterial, without much by way of sequential shape or location that is open to retrieval; once formulated, they may be retrievable only in bits and pieces. It is not easy, but not impossible, to expound them in a "logical" order so that others can follow the argument systematically. It is not easy to reorder those thoughts once they have been thought unless one is dealing with a narrative that has a definite sequential structure. Equally, one can plan out future action, which again embodies a distinct sequencing. But thinking of a more abstract kind poses problems.

With spoken as distinct from silent thoughts, there is the possibility of interaction with another interlocutor, but one has little enough time to consider and reconsider what one is thinking. One is either preprogrammed or hesitant. With writing, however, one is constantly interacting systematically with oneself over an indefinite period, in a manner that is much more difficult to sustain in silent thought or in the spoken discourse that occurs in oral cultures (in written cultures such oral procedures are influenced by the written). As a start, one may take up the thoughts of others at the point to which they have been developed in writing. That process gives rise to a consciously developing branch of knowledge, one with a recorded history, which may or may not be cumulative—that depends on the particular branch and on the methods or approach—but is always accumulating.

One has a similar experience with the development of one's own thoughts. In the course of preparing this chapter, I abandoned the writing of it a number of times, for short periods because the kettle was boiling, for longer periods to turn to another task. At each point I could return to what I was doing, review what I had written, modify my argument or my expression, then pick up where I had left off and continue the discussion, in principle cumulatively as well as accumulatively, that is, geometrically rather than arithmetically.

I have referred to a very ordinary experience in order to make a point about the nature of social and cognitive differences and development. In Lévy-Bruhl's view of the difference between simple and complex societies, there was a gap in mentalities. In much sociological thinking, the gap in outcomes is recognized (for example, in the notion of phases of social development, such as preindustrial, preliterate, and others) while the gap in mentalities is rejected; at that level diffuse relativism or extreme culturalism puts aside developmental questions as meaningless, uninteresting, or irrelevant.

There is no gap in mental ability, although we may have to allow for some genetic differences in very specific abilities, as we do in other physiological matters, such as the sickle-cell trait. Evidence of this is provided by the transformation that is taking place every day in Africa of "tribal" children into academics, research workers, and civil servants. But the transformation eludes explanations that confine themselves to an examination of one culture alone, denying not so much societally specific differences but the significance of more widespread differences. One solution lies in between. Abilities remain the same (though in the much longer term they could be affected), but outcomes differ. The explanation lies at the level of capacities that are affected by the tools one is using. Change those tools, by means of education, economy, religion, or politics, and you change the outcomes. It is not because we are intellectually better endowed in abilities that we not only live in but can operate within the kind of highly developed societies in which we find ourselves, nor yet because we are at the mercy of purely economic forces, on one hand, or highly specific cultural ones, on the other. It is partly the modes of communication that we or our societies have adopted that increase our capacities (as individuals, as agents) to understand and manipulate our world. For example, in some form or other the accountant is intrinsic to the development of the modern economy, just as measurement, whether graphic, numeric, or so on, is intrinsic to the development of the hard sciences. Those sciences are hard because they do measure and measure precisely, just as accountants have more or less precise measurements of profit and loss. That is a function of writing—not something that follows automatically, but something that requires writing as a prerequisite. In this sense, then, I describe writing as a technology of the intellect, though this phrase would apply to all means of communication to varying degrees. Language itself has its own procedures, but here I have been concerned with writing, the importance of which in the accumulation of knowledge is indicated by the typewriter or word processor in the room of every scholar, by the innumerable libraries that surround us, by the time spent in silent communication (but communication nonetheless) over books and blank sheets of paper. For all this, writing is a prerequisite, a prerequisite for the development of the technologies with which our intellect engages.

9
Power and the Book

This book has had two aims: first, to try to elaborate certain problems arising from earlier work on the influence of writing on human society, and second, to stress the power of the text. In the new nations of the world, especially in Africa, one had to be able to read and write to participate fully in the political system, since activities turned around bills, decrees, order papers, agendas—all the paraphernalia of government and administration. This instrument of power meant that nonreaders were disempowered, as in the past were whole societies.

A discussion of the problem of the power and dominance of modes of communication must be built upon an appreciation of the dynamic dimension both between and within societies. Since writing was first invented, there has always been the problem of the interface between societies with and without—the articulation of modes of communication, to adapt an Althusserian expression, although it has more frequently been a clash of cultures. There is also the changing internal position of oral and written traditions, with the greater cumulative power of the latter tending to swamp the former. Finally, there is the aspect of performance along different channels in different registers, which changes in the course of our individual development (that is, ontogenetically) as well as in that of the development of cultures (phylogenetically).

Looked at from the standpoint of the cultural history of the world we live in, there are many aspects to the domination of literate cultures. Even without the use of arms, Hindu India, that improbable candidate for cultural colonialism, had spread its tentacles into a large part of Southeast Asia, giving it the name of Indochina, as well as into the Indonesian peninsula, reproducing there highly specific cultural forms, so that in terms of written myths the great sculptures of Angkor Wat are fully comprehensible along with their counterparts in the graphic arts, the painted cotton cloths that migrated along with Homo legens. The Buddhist diaspora took similar forms, so that it does not surprise, but really should, to hear Sanskritic mantras being recited in temples in Taipei and Nara, or to find highly intelligent Japanese and Chinese scholars both working in an academic culture of world dimensions and carrying around sutras that they cannot understand, even if they can decipher them.

But it was this very presence, including the uncomprehended as well as the comprehended, that not only colonized Eastern oral cultures but provided some kind of a resistance to the cultural colonization of the West. Contrast the cultural penetration of Europe into largely oral Africa. At least at the level of their new elites, it reaches down almost to the roots of their social life, to the forms of cultivated social interaction, which is why the inhabitants of Anglophone and Francophone nations differ as much as they do, even where ethnically they are identical; the former favor beer, tea, porridge, the latter wine, coffee, omelettes, and baguettes. This example is not as trivial as it might appear. One can consider, too, major achievements in the African novel composed in metropolitan languages, including Wole Soyinka's novels written in English (for which he received a Nobel prize) and works in French such as Ferdinand Oyono's *Une Vie de boy*.

Obviously I am not saying that Africa has no culture of its own. In some respects those cultures are more flexible and varied, partly because in some domains they are more generative, less authoritative, than written ones. But they are also more vulnerable to penetration from outside and particularly to the hegemonic penetration of written cultures, even in those spheres in which writing does not have any apparent edge on oral communication; this is the phenomenon to which others have called attention in accounts of the "global village." Culturally, literate societies provided more resistance to outside domination, even in a political sense, than others, and this was not simply a matter of the latter's technological backwardness in other spheres. While it would be a mistake to overemphasize the hegemonic nature of written cultures, whether Christian, Hindu, Confucian, or any other, the nature of the kind of cultural dominance they display in relation to oral cultures or oral traditions, and the extent of their sway in geographical and historical terms, is linked to modes of communication.

There is also the intrasocietal dimension. For the first five thousand years of written cultures, during which time enormous advances were made, only a relatively small percentage of any population was able to read and write. To this extent the rest were in some ways in the power of the literates as far as important cultural activities were concerned. The same applies today in much of the world. Villagers in contemporary Africa are now divided into those who can read and write and those who cannot. It is true that at an idealized level the latter are seen as having access to different but comparable aspects of human knowledge, the depth of traditional lore being balanced against the breadth of a generalized understanding from books. But in fact the imbalance is apparent in the way that literacy is associated with power in the political, occupational, and economic domains. Moreover, an understanding of this inequality is well appreciated by those who cannot get direct access to those forms of human knowledge because they do not have control over the essential techniques. Indeed, they literally do not have the language of potential discourse, whether English or French; they are culturally dyslexic, since the national culture is diglossic. In America the view of an ex-slave such as Frederick Douglass emphasizes the point; in a context of the domination of whites with a written culture over blacks involved with the oral tradition, literacy was looked on by Douglass as the way out of the slaves' brutish condition, the path to freedom. This emerges in the respect accorded to those who "know book" as leaders of protest and revolt, in Haiti, Bahia, and elsewhere. We may object to this self-image; we may be led to advocate, as Cole and I have tried to do, that more attention be paid even in our own societies to oral achievement among the young, if only to avoid the problems caused by dyslexia and by socially induced forms of aversion to literacy with all their political and personal consequences. Nevertheless, the literate mode is inevitably seen to open up opportunities, which is why the leaders of independent African states have been so keen on universal education.

Changes in modes of communication do matter and have fundamentally altered the life of mankind. However, a new means of communication such as writing does not replace what goes before, since it is based on language; one mode supplements rather than replaces another. It is the same with the audiovisual mode, which some talk about as if it were *la fin du livre*. It is nothing of the sort. The number of books being published is forever increasing; the number of copies of newspapers sold is rising. In Britain the appearance of plays on television led to greater purchases of books associated with the broadcast. Parents still want their children to learn to speak, which they do in the home, and to read, which they do largely at school, and these activities will never be replaced, though they may be changed and even aided by audiovisual materials. What has parents of primary-school children worried is whether their children will acquire the ability to read and write (and calculate) adequately. There is little change in views about the value of books among parents who are concerned about their children's achievement in later life, and that judgment seems to me entirely realistic. The book empowers.

So the book is clearly an important instrument of power, and it is quite understandable that one sixteenth-century poet in England declared the pen to be more powerful than the sword. The extension of political domination in the major empires of Europe and Asia has always been associated with the extension of the written word and the establishment of archives and libraries. What comes to mind is obviously the extension of colonial power through not only military conquest but the spread of Religions of the Book and the establishment of schools. There are many European examples, but I prefer to take that of China, which was more secular in tone, whereas for Europe religion was often the driving force. The extension of the boundaries of the Chinese empire was closely associated with the extension of the Chinese script to tribal peoples, with the establishment of schools where locals could learn to read the same books as the Han population themselves. Local custom has often given way to national law in a most dramatic fashion, not in every context but in many significant ways. That is the same with the writings of Confucius, which provide a national ideology stretching over the same huge tract of territory in a manner that would be impossible without the book and its authority.

It is difficult to understand this process, which is not entirely hegemonic, unless one understands the attraction of the book for many of those who do not have it because they are either nonliterate or illiterate. For example, when Cyprian Equiano, an Ibo slave from West Africa, was taken to England by his master, he was brought to church to hear the master read the lesson. When Equiano got the opportunity to be in church alone, he approached the Holy Book and put his ear close to its pages so he could hear what was being said. In the oral cultures of northern Ghana I have recorded a number of instances, including divination and amulets, in which a book is held to have a magical or divine power of its own. It is a powerful object, and too close an acquaintance with it can drive a man to madness.

The case of Equiano links the power of the book with Religions of the Book, and the extension and domination of those religions occurred sometimes in conjunction with the political powers and sometimes on their own. It has frequently been religious pressure that has led to conversion and alphabetization, so that new members of the church can read the word of God. Religion often produced what one can call a "restricted literacy," concentrating upon the Qur'an or the Bible. But such instruction is virtually bound to lead to an opening up of the horizons of at least some of the population, since it enables them to consult secular works in the same language and script. It is difficult entirely to circumscribe what people should read once they have been given the tools and acquired the skills. Some may feel obliged to follow the Papal Index; others will use their abilities to read the skeptics as well as the believers.

While writing and the book can supplement the oral, they may also lead to a change in its role, and to disempowering those who depend solely upon it. That certainly happened with the introduction of the written register for land in hitherto oral societies, a process that meant focusing the claims on the one person to whom the deed was allotted and excluding from consideration the rights of other kinfolk who had claims on the same parcel. In northern Ghana the advent of tractors and of extensive mechanical rice farming led to the registration of land (demanded as security by the loan agencies) and consequently the cancellation of lineage rights. That annulment in turn led to attacks on the big farmers, whose rice was burned and machinery damaged. A similar expropriation occurred among Native Americans and again with the enclosures of common land in Western Europe, where the written law did away with customary (largely oral) usage. I do not suggest for one moment that we can abandon the written registration of land, but we should be conscious of what is happening and do our best to mitigate the consequences for those who are being disempowered by the introduction of the book. And, of course, it is precisely to avoid such disempowerment that we find such a strong movement in favor of universal literacy.

As a source of power, the book has also been very much subject to power. The history of writing can hardly be dissociated from the history of censorship, either of the blatant kind exercised directly by the organs of power, or of the more insidious kind, self-censorship, when authors or publishers (whose interests may be opposed) themselves anticipate the wishes of outside forces, whether of their own patrons (if that kind of support or protection is needed) or of more general political pressures. Then, too, there is the actual destruction of books that have already been published: the book burning of the Nazi period or the lists of forbidden reading that characterized the Catholic Church and Communist Europe. Happily, we may think, those times are behind us. But are they? The case of Salman Rushdie shows only too clearly how the influence of church and state on publications can affect not only one country but the world at large. Nor, unfortunately, is that case completely isolated. Take an incident in which I myself have recently been involved, that of the Greek-born Dr. Anastasia Karakasidou, an anthropologist who now teaches at the State University of New York at Stony Brook. She carried out ethnographic research for her doctorate in the northern part of Greece known as Macedonia and bordering on the Republic of Macedonia, which is largely Slavic. The Greek government has vigorously opposed the right of this republic to that name and as a matter of policy has denied the existence of Slavic Macedonian minorities in the country and sought to Hellenize the region both linguistically and culturally. Right and left have made common cause in the pursuit of nationalism.

When Dr. Karakasidou first presented the results of her research in 1993, she received various threats, supposedly from Greek extremists. She went ahead with her manuscript nevertheless and submitted it for publication to a series of anthropological works produced by Cambridge University Press. The manuscript was reviewed in the usual way and the readers recommended it for publication. However, when the senior management of the press heard about the earlier threats, they became worried about possible reactions from those sources and consulted their representative in Athens as well as the staff of the British embassy there. The British authorities in Athens predicted that reaction could vary from "public criticism" to "protests and demonstration, or violence or threat of violence against the author or publishers" (*London Evening Standard,* 2 February 1996). It also seems possible that account was taken of the damage that might have been done to the lucrative revenues received by another university body, the Local Examinations Syndicate, which holds some eight hundred thousand English examinations in Greece every year.

As a result, the senior management of the press recommended to the syndics, the academic body appointed by the university, that no contract be given for the book, a decision that has led to continuous protests on the part of the academics connected with the series. Reaction in Britain can be summed up in a headline from the normally right-wing *London Evening Standard,* which read, "Cambridge Bans New Book over Terrorism Fears," bringing the whole university into the affair. The publishers of books have a particular responsibility not to engage in such censorship, even if this means withdrawing personnel they consider in danger or sacrificing the loss of revenue. The alternative is much worse, especially for a university publisher, yet the policy of "publish and be damned" is absolutely essential for those dealing with the kind of recalcitrant minorities to which anthropologists are so often attached.

Let me turn to a related aspect of the role of the book relative to power, namely, the giving of power to the powerless. Recently empowerment is what great public libraries are about. Originally they were archives of the powerful, the state or church, particularly in manuscript cultures, where the number of copies of books was very limited. Each center of learning had to have its own collection, hence the great libraries of the monasteries and, since the twelfth century, of the universities in Europe. The eighteenth century saw the establishment of commercial libraries, then of the great central public libraries to which access was the democratic right of any citizen. Central public libraries were followed during the course of the nineteenth century by the creation of local counterparts in every town, often assisted in the English-speaking world by charitable donors such as Andrew Carnegie (and, later, the foundation he established), whose benefactions were specifically aimed at benefiting the poor and giving them access to book learning. At a more academic level, the spread of universities, colleges, and secondary schools has meant the establishment of large collections in provincial towns, once again more so in Anglophone than in Francophone areas, where the funding of university libraries has been even less sufficient to keep pace with the growth in knowledge. However, the situation may be remedied in the future, since it is the explicit intention of the new Bibliothèque nationale de France to enable provincial libraries to gain access to the capital's great resources in books and articles by electronic means. That seems an important and indeed essential measure of empowerment of the less well endowed parts of the country. It is a possibility opened up by the cheapness, compactness, and rapidity of dissemination provided by the new electronic media. These new techniques do not at all spell the end of the book but rather the easier and wider distribution of its contents throughout the country and eventually the world. It is extraordinary to sit at my computer in a cottage in rural France and consult the catalog of the Library of Congress in Washington, D.C. It will be an even greater step forward when I can go to my local library and order electronically a copy of an article or book I need. I speak of convenience to academics, but it also means that schoolteachers, local historians, autodidacts—anyone at all—can engage in the same consultations, truly an empowerment of those who are not privileged to live within a few miles of the center of Paris.

Public libraries represent a socialization of the book, the communal ownership of the means of communication, making its contents available to all who can read and write. Obviously the empowerment the book can bestow depends upon the capacity to read and write, and it is virtually only in the last hundred years that literacy has been available to the larger part of any nation. Before that, while those who could not read and write had no direct access to the book, their lives were obviously greatly influenced by it, in both religious and secular terms.

It was the desire to give the populace direct access to the Scriptures, rather than any Enlightenment program to relieve the masses of their darkness in a secular sense, that led Protestants, and later the Counter-Reformation, to attempt to achieve more widespread literacy. In England Sunday schools were instrumental in spreading literacy among the working classes; in France the convents were important, and much early schooling centered upon the catechism. So too in Islam learning to read and write was primarily a matter of mastering religious texts, as it was in Hinduism. Secular schools multiplied during the eighteenth century (although earlier in Holland and England we find the grammar schools), and there was certainly a significant extension of the reading public that was intimately associated with the rise of the novel.

That rise was less concerned with the laboring classes than with the petty bourgeoisie and with the creation of commercial libraries by booksellers, who lent their stock out to those who could not afford to buy them—and in the eighteenth century the price was still high relative to incomes. Interestingly, the larger part of this audience was female, for women had greatly benefited from the extension of literacy in this period and it was with them that the new popular genre of the novel was especially associated.

In the early history of the book in Western Europe, women had little role to play. Initially schooling in reading and writing was generally for men, who played the major priestly and administrative roles. Nevertheless, some women became literate, and convents were one of the principal sites for the learning of letters. Until at least the ninth century their education was largely limited to "a solid knowledge of the Bible, the works of the fathers of the church and some acquaintance with canon and civil law." But these institutions had libraries; when Anglo-Saxon missionaries went to the Continent in the early eighth century they continued to correspond with nuns in England, "requesting material assistance, books and helpers." Some of the nunneries were attached to monasteries; nuns and monks had separate quarters, but in the scriptoria and the schools, "centres of civilization," they participated together in copying manuscripts (Mundy 1991: 160, 165). There were also secular schools, which taught both men and women. In Brussels in 1320, four of the ten lower schools were for girls; there were even some female teachers and scribes in the towns. Another important site of female learning was the home. Often the impetus was practical—there might be no male children to inherit family property, only females; in great estates (as in China) women might have to act as "domestic bursars" (see McDermott 1990); the wives of merchants and craftsmen often had to help with the business, or, in the case of widows, run it, and that could not be done without letters and some form of bookkeeping. Women have frequently been specifically barred from schooling, and yet such is the nature of literate activity that reading can be learned in private—by the slave from a sympathetic mistress, by a girl from her male sibling as he himself learns, by a daughter from an eccentric father or a governess. We know that this occurred over and over again, and that there have been women authors (and hence women readers) from an early period. Witness the numerous female poets of the T'ang; the female troubadours of medieval Europe (Bogin 1976); the poet Sappho in Greece; the Lady Murasaki Shikibu, author of *The Tale of Genji*, the world's first full-length novel, in eleventh-century Japan; and the many early women poets in the anthologies of southern India. Moreover, writing can be carried out without the necessity of an immediate audience, so Murasaki Shikibu could write down her memoirs (in some cases this was done under a male pseudonym) for them to reach a reading public at a much later date and even in another country.

As I have noted, in Western Europe women became identified with the novel, and especially with romances. It was partly this identification of the novel with the frivolities of women that was behind the antinovelistic prejudices of the eighteenth century, as illustrated, for example, in the works of Charlotte Lennox, especially *The Female Quixote,* or in the writings of Jean-Jacques Rousseau. The same theme continued into the nineteenth century; the adventures of Madame Bovary are intimately connected with her inability to separate life from fiction, or more broadly what she read in books. But women were authors as well as readers, and as such they were capable of commenting upon their own position as well as that of their male counterparts. Women novelists such as Jane Austen clearly changed the perception of the role of women as well as helped to reshape it.

Feminist interests soon took a more directly political turn, especially following the outbreak of the French Revolution, for example, in the work of Mary Wollstonecraft, mother of Mary Shelley, who wrote *A Vindication of the Rights of Woman* (1792), modeled on Thomas Paine's *Rights of Man* and mainly directed to education; with the struggle of Caroline Norton (the granddaughter of the playwright Richard Sheridan) to get access to her children and to change the divorce laws in England starting in the 1830s; and with the fight of American feminists such as Elizabeth Cady Stanton over marital roles about the same time. The protagonists were clearly women who knew books and were prepared to use their skills in that direction to further the cause. This was true also in the wave of feminist activity that led to the achievement of the vote, first in some American states (Wyoming in 1869), then in England in 1918, and finally in France in 1944, where in each case books and pamphlets played a very important part in the struggle. And it has been even more the case, if possible, in the more recent feminist movement of the 1960s through the 1980s. Certainly meetings, demonstrations, and other forms of political activity have been significant, but a big part has been played by the writing, publishing, and diffusion of books, especially by houses such as Virago and by women's studies departments in universities. Even when the major participants shifted from direct political action to women's history and other matters, it was the writing that remained dominant over the longer run, and it is the writing that has made an impact in a way that studies of class have never done. This change in knowledge systems (I do not speak of any associated changes in human behavior) has been achieved largely through the written word, through the book. Television and other audiovisual media have also played their part, but feminists appear there as authors rather than as presenters of the ideas via the spoken word.

Much has been written about women's exclusion in oral cultures from certain forms of male knowledge. This applies not so much to everyday activities, where women have important technological roles, but even when work is segregated by gender, women are not totally ignorant of what goes on among the men. The arrow poison of the LoDagaa of northern Ghana is brewed by men at a special cooking place outside the compound, quite separate from the inside, domestic hearth where normal food is prepared. Nevertheless, women get to know something about the ingredients that are included. In regard to more esoteric knowledge, such as that embodied in mythical recitations, the face-to-face transmission of knowledge in oral cultures means that women can be kept out in a radical and determined way. For example, the Bagre myth of the LoDagaa is divided into two parts, the White and the Black. Women can be initiated into the first stage and hear the White, but from the Black, with its elaborate account of the acquisition of mankind's culture, they are excluded. Secret societies, too, often formally exclude women from membership, at least at the senior levels. And in masquerades of one kind or another, masked males attempt to breed fear in women's minds and in those of their children. But again, in all of these cases it is my experience that it does not take women long to guess at what is happening behind the mask or in the secret groves.

As in the case of women, underprivileged classes are seen as suffering from the dominance of those who have acquired the power of the word, especially the written word, namely, the ruling classes. It is true that the powerful used literacy to support their position, elaborating a bureaucracy, promulgating laws, and giving expression to hegemonic ideologies. But for several millennia the rulers themselves were not always literate; they were rather the employers of clerks and scribes, who were especially trained for their service. That meant new professions of schoolteachers and other specialists in the written word, who were not simply passive instruments of the powers that be. They were often priests, as in Mesopotamia, Egypt, the Islamic countries, India, and medieval Europe. That is to say, they contemplated and wrote about the nature of the world, as (in more secular circumstances) did the many intellectuals who appeared in Greece. As such, they did not merely follow the dominant view of things but added an element of doubt, criticism, even opposition, pointing out the contradictions in current values

and suggesting alternative approaches. Think of the role of philosophers such as Mencius and many others in China who were critical of
the distribution of power, of food, of justice. And the same is true of
many Greek philosophers and Roman moralists; they were not simply
subservient to the authorities but elaborated their own critique.

I do not want to argue that such a kernel of doubt, of skepticism,
does not exist in embryonic form in oral societies; indeed, I have suggested just the opposite, that such doubts are often related to perceived
contradictions in the human situation and in that way are part of the
esprit humain (1997). But what writing and the book do is to make the
implicit explicit and to create a continuing tradition, not only of dominant ideologies but of critical ones as well. We see that clearly in these
various written traditions, where scholars are constantly referring back
to previous writings and using them to support their current positions.
In a rather different way we see it in relation to protest against the
dominant political system. The writings of Marx have served a similar
purpose over the last 150 years, but before that the tradition went back
to the writings that surrounded the French Revolution, or in Anglophone countries to the works of Thomas Paine and back again to the
works of the Levellers and others of the English Revolution, whose line
has been traced by British historians such as Christopher Hill and Ed-
ward Thompson.

Protest on the part of the underprivileged classes has often been connected with a movement toward universal literacy so that people would
be able to draw not only on these writings but on the general written
culture. That movement occurred most dramatically in Africa, where
the ending of colonial rule saw a great surge in education, in the attempt to give everyone the power to read and write. And it is significant that the leaders of these independence movements had already been
empowered by the book, so they could participate in the tradition of
those who in Europe had struggled for *liberté, egalité,* and *fraternité.*
That was so too with earlier revolts in the New World, where Toussaint-
Louverture in Haiti, leader of the Black Jacobins, was certainly a literate slave who had read the work of the abolitionist Abbé Raynal.
Most remarkable, perhaps, was the slave revolt in Bahia, Brazil, in
1835, which was inspired by Islam. So worried did the authorities be-

come about the power of the book in the hands of the slaves that those who could read and write were packed off back to West Africa, leaving behind the illiterates, who were less likely to engage in an effective struggle.

That history has been played out in many parts of the world, showing that the book can empower the powerless; the point lies behind much of the twentieth-century pressure toward universal literacy, whereas earlier the pressure often came from religious quarters. And that, I take it, is one of the major aims of the libraries, both great and small, which, constructed by the power of the state as well as by the generosity of rich individuals, are the expression of a democratic order that aims to empower all its citizens, the powerless as well as the powerful, women as well as men, the inhabitants of rural France as well as those of Paris.

Notes

Chapter 1. Objections and Refutations

1. Watt's work on this subject was submitted as a fellowship dissertation to St. John's College, Cambridge (Watt 1947).
2. I myself modified the argument with regard to the alphabet in Goody 1968 and in more detail in Goody 1977a, explaining that I thought we had earlier been too dependent upon Havelock's seminal work.
3. The extent to which they do reinterpret the text is an interesting question; human potentialities are indeed great, but there has to be restrictions on how far they can go.
4. The data on Dagomba come from Tait n.d.; that from Gonja is from my own field notes; for Asante, see the series of stool histories published by the Institute of African Studies, Legon, Ghana.

Chapter 2. Memory in Oral Tradition

1. In Spanish, learning by heart is identified with "*apprender de memoria*"; in German it is "*auswendig lernen,*" learning by turning things inside out.
2. On the implications for the study of myth and oral discourse generally, see Goody 1995b.
3. If we include the legendary Coming of the Kusiele from Lawra.
4. In the following transcription, italic text in square brackets is my comment.

Chapter 3. The Construction of a Ritual Text:
The Shift from Oral to Written Channels

1. In the following transcriptions of portions of the Bagre, italic text in square brackets is my comment; roman text in square brackets is uttered by the Speaker but is not considered part of the Bagre.

Chapter 4. The Time of Telling and the Telling of Time in Written and Oral Cultures

1. Briefly, a narrative involves not simply sequence but a relation between the elements involving the same characters or possibly objects.
2. I have a further discussion of these genres in relation to narrative in Goody 1997.
3. Webster's dictionary defines plot as "the main story of a literary work . . . unfolding of a carefully connected sequence of motivated incidents."
4. Contrary to E. A. Havelock's statement (1986: 28, 44) about the Bagre, I see no evidence of Muslim influence, though I have long pondered the possibility.
5. See Brooks 1987 for a perceptive account of what he calls "the oral in the written."
6. I am indebted to Bliss Carnochan for a point about remembering, and to Cindy Ward for comments about dates in *Robinson Crusoe;* in addition, the remarks of the participants at the conference at which this chapter was initially presented pointed to areas where I needed to supplement the argument, which in any case draws on my earlier writing as well as on current interests.

Chapter 5. Writing and Revolt in Bahia

1. The first slaves came to Brazil in 1549, a batch of 120 from Guinea and São Tomé, to work on the sugar plantations.
2. In mid-nineteenth-century Brazil 40 to 60 percent of the colored population was free, rising to 74 percent in the 1872 census. The comparative figure for Cuba in 1861 was 35 percent and for the United States in 1860 11 percent (Klein 1969: 36–37).
3. Runaway slaves fought against the Dutch in the northeast under the command of the free black Henrique Dias (Klein 1969: 31).
4. Among the Yoruba in Brazil these "guilds" were known as *cantos;* members pooled resources to buy freedom, with the first to secure it contributing to the pool until the last member was free (Kent 1970: 340; Pierson 1939: 530). Systems of rotating credit are well known from West Africa and are still used for accumulating funds for a large transaction that no individual felt he could afford.
5. Fox (Rio de Janeiro) to the Duke of Wellington, 11 December 1835 (FO 13/117, Public Record Office, London), for the population estimates. In 1807 the census for São Salvador showed 28 percent white, 20 percent mulatto, and 52 percent black (Russell-Wood 1982: 48).

6. The quotations from Parkinson are from his correspondence with the Duke of Wellington (FO 13/21, Public Record Office, London).

7. Muslims were known to the Yoruba as "Male," presumably from *Mali* (*Malle* in Mande), whence Islamic practices spread (cf. the Hausa term *Wangara* and the Gonja *N'sau*). Kent, however, claims the name comes from *mallam,* which structures his whole interpretation (1970: 356); the Males rebelled because their marginal religious position left them no room for adjustment. Russell-Wood (1982: 180) states that the leader of one Malinke group, known as Males in Brazil, was called *lemane* (that is, imam) and presided over marriage ceremonies. According to Johnston (1910: 94), a "considerable aggregation of slaves grew up in Bahia in the first quarter of the nineteenth century who styled themselves *Musulmi.*"

8. On the contact between Africa and Brazil, see especially the works of Verger (1964, 1968) and Cunha (1985). Pierson (1939: 528) remarks that early in the eighteenth century natives of the Guinea coast referred to the outside world as "Bahia." He also suggests that it was proximity to West Africa that led to the greater preservation of African cultural forms and to the development of Nago as a common language.

9. The translation here is by Professor Manuela Carneiro da Cunha. See also the translation by Pattee (Ramos 1956: 48–49). A similar conclusion to that of Martins and Rodrigues was reached by Etienne; Kent's rejection of the thesis (1970: 346 ff.) seems unconvincing.

10. See also Kent's comments on these papers (1970: 353). He is suspicious of all talk not only of a jihad but of the general influence of Islam; it was Rodrigues and Etienne, he claims, who invented the idea that one of the participants, Pedro Luna, was the Almamy (imam).

11. According to Kent (1970: 354), nine of the participants were repatriated. "The repatriation of Africans from Brazil was not uncommon . . . , nor was it rare for Africans of the upper caste to come to Brazil to be educated, especially in Bahia," writes Rodrigues (1965: 126), although the case to which he refers is the second wife of the famous Afro-Brazilian trader "Xaxá" Sousa, the daughter of the king of Dahomey. It has to be remembered that Brazil was closely linked to Africa until sometime between 1850 and 1858, when "the tradition of three centuries of ethnic-cultural contacts was broken" (Rodrigues 1965: 193). Exile was the fate of other slaves involved in escape or revolt. Some Yoruba slaves from Brazil were sent to Sierra Leone, and, interestingly, it was the Muslims among them who kept their own language (Banton 1957).

12. In fact, Rodrigues writes of a mosque at roughly the same time, but presumably it was not in Bahia.

13. The references are to Rodrigues 1976, Querino 1927, and Etienne 1909.

14. The figure is from Verger. According to Kent, a total of 234 reached the

final stage. Of these the Nagos, Hausa, Nupe, Ewe, and Kanuri accounted for 213; the total included 14 women. The figure I have given
are from Prince 1972.

15. On the wide range of work available to freedmen in the nineteenth century, see Klein 1969.

16. For Yoruba, see Eades 1980: 77.

17. The fraternity was founded in 1460. Black slaves came to Lisbon from
the north coast of Mauritania in 1441; by the 1450s the annual figure
was between seven hundred and eight hundred, and by 1551 approxi-
mately 10 percent of the population of Lisbon consisted of blacks. Corporations of artisans were founded in the twelfth century, and these led
to confraternities (Saint-Léon 1941; Monti 1927).

18. As shown in the illustration to Denham et al. 1966: 471.

19. The chief of police was often a lawyer and hence might set his sights on
further objectives of a political kind.

20. I cannot stress too strongly that in speaking of oral religions, I am talking only about oral cultures, where writing is absent. On the other hand,
an oral tradition and oral transmission clearly do persist in societies with
writing.

21. I am heavily indebted to Professor Manuela Carneiro da Cunha, formerly of the University of São Paulo, presently of the University of
Chicago, for discussion, references, and the use of the library, as well as
to John Iliffe in Cambridge. My interest in the role of literacy among
African slaves was stimulated by the work of E. Genovese and I. Wilks;
in Brazil, which I visited courtesy of the British Council and the Depart-
ment of Psychology of the University of Pernambuco; and by various
colleagues and friends in Recife, Campinas, São Paulo, and Rio de
Janeiro. The last part of the paper is a brief summary of my discussion
of religion in *The Logic of Writing and the Organisation of Society*
(1986a).

Chapter 6. Derrida among the
Archives of the Written and the Oral

1. "What was the meaning of my lecture last night on the training of ana-
lysts? . . . It is essential to carefully distinguish between symbolism properly so-called, that is, symbolism as structured in language, that in which
we understand one another here, and natural symbolism. I have summed
this up in the epigram, to read coffee-grounds is not to read hieroglyphics"
(Lacan 1995: 195).

2. See, for example, the use of *débordement* (Johnson 1993: 151).

References

Adams, R.
1996   *Paths of Fire: An Anthropologist's Inquiry into Western Technology*. Princeton, N.J.

Axton, R.
1974   *European Drama of the Early Middle Ages*. London.

Baines, J.
1983   Literacy and Ancient Egyptian Society. *Man* n.s. 18: 572–99.

Banton, M. P.
1957   *West African City: A Study of Tribal Life in Freetown*. London.

Baron, G.
1981   *Mémoire vivante: Vie et oeuvre de Marcel Jousse*. Paris.

Barth, F.
1987   *Cosmologies in the Making: A Generative Approach to Cultural Variation in Inner New Guinea*. Cambridge.

Bartlett, F. C.
1932   *Remembering*. Cambridge.

Biebuyck, D. P.
1969   *The Mwindo Epic from the Banyanga (Congo Republic)*. Berkeley.

Bogin, M.
1976   *The Woman Troubadours*. New York.

Bohannan, L.
1952   A Genealogical Charter. *Africa* 22: 301–15.

Bottéro, J.
1977   Les noms du Marduk, l'écriture et la "logique" en Mésopotamie ancienne. In M. de Jong Ellis, ed., *Essays on the Ancient Near East in Memory of Jacob Joel Finkelstein*. Hamden, Conn.

Bowra, C. M.
1962   *Primitive Song*. London.
Bowser, F. P.
1974   *The African Slave in Colonial Peru, 1524–1650*. Stanford.
Braimah, J. A.
n.d.   *Gonja Drums*. Accra.
Brazil, P. T. I.
1909   Os Mâles. *Revista do Instituto Historico e Geografico Brasiliero* 120, 72: 67–126.
Brennan, T.
1993   *History after Lacan*. Cambridge.
Britto, E. A. de Caldas
1903   Levantos de pretos na Bahia. *Revista do Instituto Geographico e Historico de Bahia* 29: 69–90.
Brooks, P.
1987   The Storyteller. *Yale Journal of Criticism* 1: 21–38.
Candler, J., and W. Burgess
1853   *Narrative of a Recent Visit to Brazil*. London.
Chadwick, H. M.
1912   *The Heroic Age*. Cambridge.
Chambers, E. K.
1903   *The Mediaeval Stage*. Oxford.
Childe, G.
1942   *What Happened in History*. Harmondsworth.
Clanchy, M. T.
1979   *From Memory to Written Record: England 1066–1300*. London.
Cole, H.
1967   *Christophe: King of Haiti*. London.
Cole, M., J. Gay, J. A. Glick, and D. W. Sharpe
1971   *The Cultural Context of Learning and Thinking*. New York.
Culler, J.
1979   Jacques Derrida. In J. Sturrock, ed., *Structuralism and Since: From Lévi-Strauss to Derrida*. Oxford.
Cunha, M. Carneiro da
1985   *Negros, estrangeiros: Os escravos libertos et sua volta à Africa*. São Paulo.
Defoe, D.
1927   *The Life and Strange Adventures of Robinson Crusoe of*
[1719]   *York, Mariner*. Oxford.

Denham, D., H. Clapperton, and W. Oudney
1966   Narrative of Travels and Discoveries in Northern and
[1826]   Central Africa in the Years 1822, 1823 and 1824. Ed. E. W.
         Bovill. Cambridge.
Derrida, J.
1974   Of Grammatology. Trans. G. Spivak. Baltimore.
1978a   Freud and the Scene of Writing. In Writing and Difference.
         London.
1978b   Writing and Difference. London.
Dewdney, S.
1975   The Sacred Scrolls of the Southern Ojibway. Toronto.
Douglas, M.
1966   Purity and Danger. London.
Eades, J. S.
1980   The Yoruba Today. Cambridge.
Edwards, W. A. L. (ed. and trans.)
1911   The Mishna on Idolatry 'Aboda Zara. Cambridge.
Eisenstein, E. L.
1979   The Printing Press as an Agent of Change: Communications
         and Cultural Transformations in Early Modern Europe.
         2 vols. Cambridge.
Elias, N.
1978   The Civilizing Process. Oxford.
Etienne, I.
1909   La Secte musulmane des Malès du Bresil et leur révolte en
         1835. Anthropos (Basel) 4: 99–105, 405–15.
Ferreira, J. C.
1903   As insurreções dos Africanos na Bahia. Revista do Instituto
         Geographico e Historico de Bahia 29: 90–114.
1909   Os Mâles. Revista do Instituto Historico e Geographico
         Brasiliero 42.
Fielding, H.
1808   The History of the Life of the Late Mr. Jonathan Wild the
[1743]   Great. London.
1950   The History of Tom Jones, a Foundling. New York.
[1749]
Finnegan, R.
1970   Oral Literature in Africa. Oxford.
1973   The Great Divide. In R. Horton and R. Finnegan, eds.,
         Modes of Thought: Essays on Thinking in Western and
         Non-Western Societies. London.

1977   *Oral Poetry: Its Nature, Significance, and Social Context.* Cambridge.

Freud, S.

1984   A Note upon the "Mystic Writing Pad." *Standard Edition*
[1925]   *of the Complete Psychological Works of Sigmund Freud,* vol. 19. London.

Freyre, G.

1946   *The Masters and the Slaves.* New York.
[1933]

Friedemann, N. de, and R. Cross

1979   *Ma Ngombe: Guerreros y ganaderos en Palenque.* Bogota.

Fuller, C.

1984   *Servants of the Goddess: The Priests of a South Indian Temple.* Cambridge.

Gandah, S. W. D. K., and J. Goody

1995   Variations of the Bagre. St. John's College, University of Cambridge. Photocopied.

Genovese, E. D.

1981   *From Rebellion to Revolution: Afro-American Slave Re-*
[1979]   *volts in the Making of the New World.* New York.

Giddens, A.

1991   *Modernity.* Cambridge.

Gluckman, M.

1955a   *Custom and Conflict in Africa.* Oxford.
1955b   *The Judicial Process among the Barotse of Northern Rhodesia.* Manchester.
1965   *The Ideas of Barotse Jurisprudence.* New Haven.

Goldman, R. P.

1991   Introduction. In P. S. Jaini, *Gender and Salvation: Jaina Debates on the Spiritual Liberation of Women.* Berkeley.

Goody, E.

1972   *Contexts of Kinship: An Essay in the Family Sociology of the Gonja of Northern Ghana.* Cambridge.
1995   Anticipatory Interactive Planning. In E. Goody, ed., *Social Intelligence and Interaction.* Cambridge.
Forthcoming *The Drum Titles of Gonja.*

Goody, E. (ed.)

1978   *Questions and Politeness: Strategies in Social Interaction.* Cambridge.

Goody, J.

1954   The Ethnography of the Northern Territories of the Gold

Coast, West of the White Volta. Colonial Office, London. Mimeographed.

1956   *The Social Organisation of the Lo Wiili.* London.

1957   Anomie in Ashanti? *Africa* 27: 75–104.

1961   Religion and Ritual: The Definitional Problem. *British Journal of Sociology* 12: 142–64.

1962   *Death, Property and the Ancestors.* Stanford.

1968a   Time: Social Organisation. In D. L. Sills, ed., *International Encyclopedia of the Social Sciences.* New York.

1968b   Restricted Literacy in Northern Ghana. In J. Goody, ed., *Literacy in Traditional Societies.* Cambridge.

1970   Reform, Renewal and Resistance: A Mahdi in Northern Ghana. In C. Allen and R. W. Johnson, eds., *African Perspectives: Papers in the History, Politics, and Economics of Africa Presented to Thomas Hodgkin.* Cambridge.

1971   The Impact of Islamic Writing on the Oral Cultures of West Africa. *Cahiers d'Etudes Africaines* 11: 455–66.

1972   *The Myth of the Bagre.* Oxford.

1975a   Religion, Social Change, and the Sociology of Conversion. In J. Goody, ed., *Changing Social Structure in Ghana.* London.

1975b   Schools, Education, and the Social System: Some Utopian Suggestions. *Interchange* (Toronto) 6: 1–5.

1976   *Production and Reproduction: A Comparative Study of the Domesic Domain.* Cambridge.

1977a   *The Domestication of the Savage Mind.* Cambridge.

1977b   Mémoire et apprentissage dans les sociétés avec et sans écriture: La transmission du Bagré. *L'Homme* 17: 29–52.

1977c   Against Ritual: Loosely Structured Thoughts on a Loosely Defined Topic. In S. Falk Moore and B. Myerhoff, eds., *Secular Ritual.* 2 vols. Amsterdam.

1982   Decolonisation in Africa: National Politics and Village Politics. *Cambridge Anthropology* 7: 2–24.

1983   *The Development of the Family and Marriage in Europe.* Cambridge.

1986a   *The Logic of Writing and the Organisation of Society.* Cambridge.

1986b   Writing, Religion and Revolt in Bahia. *Visible Language* 20: 318–43.

1987   *The Interface between the Written and the Oral.* Cambridge.

1993   *The Culture of Flowers.* Cambridge.

1995a	*The East in the West*. Cambridge.
1995b	The Anthropologist and the Tape-recorder. *Minpaku Anthropology Newsletter* (Osaka).
1996	Cognitive Contradictions and Universals: Creation and Evolution in Oral Cultures (The Frazer Lecture, 1994, Liverpool). *European Journal of Social Anthropology* 4: 1–16.
1997	*Representations and Contradictions: Ambivalence towards Images, Theatre, Fiction, Relics, and Sexuality*. Oxford.

Goody, J. (ed.)

1968	*Literacy in Traditional Societies*. Cambridge.

Goody, J., and C. Duly

1981	Studies in the Use of Computers in Social Anthropology. Report to the [British] Social Science Research Council, HR 5725/1.

Goody, J., and S. W. D. K. Gandah

1981	*Une Récitation du Bagré*. Paris.

Goody, J., and I. P. Watt

1963	The Consequence of Literacy. *Comparative Studies in Society and History* 5: 304–45.

Greenway, J.

1964	*Literature among the Primitives*. Hatboro, Penn.

Halbwachs, M.

1925	*Les Cadres sociaux de la mémoire*. Paris.

Harrison, J.

1914	*Ancient Art and Ritual*. London.

Havelock, E. A.

1963	*Preface to Plato*. Cambridge, Mass.
1986	*The Muse Learns to Write: Reflections on Orality and Literacy from Antiquity to the Present*. New Haven.

Haynes, D. E., and G. Prakash

1991	*Contesting Power: Resistance and Everyday Social Relations in South Asia*. Oxford.

Hocket, C. F.

1960	The Origins of Speech. *Scientific American* 203: 88–106.

Hone, J.

1942	*W. B. Yeats*. London.

Hooke, S. H. (ed.)

1933	*Myth and Ritual: Essays on the Myth and Ritual of the Hebrews in Relation to the Culture Pattern of the Ancient East*. London.

1958   *Myth, Ritual, and Kingship: Essays on the Theory and Practice of Kingship in the Ancient Near East and in Israel.* Oxford.

Jacoby, F.
1923   *Die Fragmente der Griechischen Historiker*, vol. 1, *Genealogie und Mythographie*. Berlin.
1949   *Atthis*. Oxford.

James, C. L. R.
1938   *The Black Jacobins: Toussaint Louverture and the San Domingo Revolution*. London.

Johnson, C.
1993   *System and Writing in the Philosophy of Jacques Derrida*. Cambridge.

Johnston, H. H.
1910   *The Negro in the New World*. London.

Kane, P. V.
1930–62   *History of Dharmaśāstra*. 5 vols. Poona.

Kent, R. K.
1970   African Revolt in Bahia: 24–25 January 1835. *Journal of Social History* 3: 334–56.

Kellogg, R.
1973   Oral Literature. *New Literary History* 5: 55–66.

Kirk, G. S.
1970   *Myth: Its Meaning and Function in Ancient and Other Cultures*. Cambridge.

Klein, H. S.
1969   The Coloured Freedmen in Brazilian Slave Society. *Journal of Social History* 3: 30–32.

Koster, H.
1816   *Travels in Brazil*. London.

Lacan, J.
1995   *The Seminar of Jacques Lacan*, book 3, *The Psychoses*. Ed.
[1981]   J. A. Miller.

Last, M.
1967   *The Sokoto Caliphate*. London.

Leavis, Q. D.
1932   *Fiction and the Reading Public*. London.

Le Goff, J.
1984   *The Birth of Purgatory*. Trans. A. Goldhammer. Chicago.
[1981]

Lévi-Strauss, C.
    1962   *La Pensée sauvage*. Paris.
    1964–71   *Mythologiques*. 4 vols. Paris.
    1968   *Structural Anthropology*. London.
Lévy-Bruhl, L.
    1910   *Les Fonctions mentales dans les sociétés inférieures*. Paris.
Lord, A. B.
    1964   *The Singer of Tales*. Cambridge, Mass.
McDermott, J.
    1990   The Chinese Domestic Bursar. *Asian Cultural Studies* 2:
                15–32.
McKeon, M.
    1987   *The Origins of the English Novel, 1600–1740*. Baltimore.
McLuhan, M.
    1962   *The Gutenberg Galaxy: The Making of Typographic Man*.
                Toronto.
Meyerowitz, E. L. R.
    1951   *The Sacred State of the Akan*. London.
Mintz, S. W.
    1985   *Sweetness and Power: The Place of Sugar in the Modern
                World*. New York.
Monteil, V.
    1967   Analyse des 25 documents arabes des Malès de Bahia
                (1835). *Bulletin de l'Institut fondamental d'Afrique noire*
                29: 94–95.
Monti, G. M.
   ˙ 1927   *Le confraternite medievali dell'alta e media Italia*. 2 vols.
                Venice.
Mundy, J. H.
    1991   *Europe in the High Middle Ages, 1150–1309*. London.
Nakamura, H.
    1964   *Ways of Thinking of Eastern Peoples: India—China—
                Tibet—Japan*. Honolulu.
Needham, J.
    1986   *Science and Civilisation in China*, vol. 6, *Biology and Bio-
                logical Technology*, part 1, *Botany*. Cambridge.
Neisser, U.
    1982   *Memory Observed: Remembering in Natural Contexts*.
                New York.
Olson, D.
    1994   *The World on Paper*. Cambridge.

Ong, W. J.
1974   *Ramus, Method, and the Decay of Dialogue.* New York.
[1958]
Palmer, H. R.
1928   *Sudanese Memoirs, I.* Lagos.
Parry, J.
1984   The Text in Context. London School of Economics.
                Photocopied.
Parry, J. H., and P. M. Sherlock
1965   *A Short History of the West Indies.* 2nd ed. London.
Parry, M.
1930   Studies in the Epic Technique of Oral Verse-making. 1.
                Homer and Homeric Style. *Harvard Studies in Classical
                Philology* 41: 73–147, 43: 1–50.
Pelliot, P.
1953   *Les Débats de l'imprimérie en Chine.* Paris.
Phillips, T. (ed.)
1995   *Africa: The Art of a Continent.* London.
Pierson, D.
1939   The Negro in Bahia, Brazil. *American Sociological Review*
                4: 524–33.
Pollock, R.
1979   The Influence of Brukung on the Social Organisation of the
                Shiare. Ph.D. dissertation, University of Cambridge.
Prain, G. D.
1984   Respecting Power: Temples, Resources and Authority in
                Southern Tamilnadu, India. Ph.D. dissertation, University
                of Cambridge.
Price, R.
1973   *Maroon Societies: Rebel Slave Communities in the Ameri-
                cas.* New York.
Prince, H.
1972   Slave Rebellion in Bahia, 1807–1835. Ph.D. dissertation,
                Columbia University.
Querino, M.
1927   A raça Africana e sens costumes na Baia. *Revista de
                Academia Brasileira de Letras* 25, 69: 126–28; 25, 70:
                131–99.
Ramos, A.
1956   *The Negro in Brazil.* Trans. R. F. Pattee. Rio de Janeiro.
[1934]

Rattray, R. S.
1923   *Ashanti.* London.
1927   *Religion and Art in Ashanti.* Oxford.
1929   *Ashanti Law and Constitution.* Oxford.
Rawski, E. S.
1979   *Education and Popular Literacy in Ch'ing China.* Ann
            Arbor, Mich.
Reefe, T.
1977   Lukasa: A Luba Memory Device. *African Arts* 10: 48–
            50, 88.
1981   *The Rainbow and the Kings: A History of the Luba Empire
            to 1891.* Berkeley.
Reichert, R. P.
1967   L'insurrection d'esclaves de 1835 à la lumière des docu-
            ments arabes des Archives publiques de l'Etat de Bahia
            (Brésil). *Bulletin de l'Institut fondamental d'Afrique noire*
            29: 99–140.
Reichert, R. P., and A. B. Abdelghani
1966   Os documentos àrabes do arquivo do Estado da Bahia.
            Afro-Asia (University of Bahia) 2, 213: 169–76.
Reis, J. J.
1976   A elite Baiana face os movimentos sociaias, Bahia, 1824–
            1840. *Revista de História São Paulo* 108: 341–84.
1978   Black Revolts in Bahia, 1807–1835. M.A. thesis, University
            of Minnesota.
Riesman, D.
1956   *The Oral Tradition, the Written Word, the Screen Image.*
            Yellow Springs, Oh.
Rivers, W. H. R.
1912   The Disappearance of Useful Arts. In *Festskrift Tillägnad
            Edvard Westermarck.* Helsingfors.
Rodrigues, J. H.
1965   *Brazil and Africa.* Berkeley.
Rodrigues, N.
1932   *Os Africanos nos Brazil.* São Paulo.
Rout, L. B., Jr.
1976   *The African Experience in Spanish America: 1502 to the
            Present Day.* Cambridge.
Russell-Wood, A. J. R.
1968   *Fidalgos and Philanthropists: The Santa Casa da Misericor-
            dia of Bahia, 1550–1755.* London.

1982   *The Black Man in Slavery and Freedom in Colonial Brazil.* London.

Saint-Léon, M.
1941   *Histoire des corporations de métiers depuis leurs origines jusqu'à leurs suppression en 1791.* 4th ed. Paris.

Schmandt-Bessarat, D.
1992   *Before Writing.* Austin, Tex.

Schuler, M.
1970   Ethnic Slave Rebellions in the Caribbean and the Guianas. *Journal of Social History* 3: 374–85.

Schwartz, S. B.
1970   The Mocambo: Slave Resistance in Colonial Bahia. *Journal of Social History* 3: 315–33.

Scribner, S., and M. Cole
1981   *The Psychology of Literacy.* Cambridge, Mass.

Sharp, W. F.
1976   *Slavery on the Spanish Frontier: The Colombian Chocó, 1610–1810.* Norman, Okla.

Smith, R.
1966   On the White Yajurveda Vaṃśa. *East and West* 16: 112–25.

Smith, W. R.
1889   *Lectures on the Religion of the Semites.* Edinburgh.

Soyinka, W.
1990   *Myth, Literature and the African World.* Cambridge.
[1976]

Steiner, R.
1995   "Et in Arcadia ego?": Some Notes on Methodological Issues in the Use of Psychoanalytic Documents and Archives. *International Journal of Psychoanalysis* 76: 39–58.

Sterne, L.
1965   *The Life and Opinions of Tristram Shandy, Gentleman.* Boston, Mass.
[1760]

Stone, L.
1979   The Revival of Narrative: Reflections on a New Old History. *Past and Present* 85: 3–24.

Street, B.
1984   *Literacy in Theory and Practice.* Cambridge.

Tait, D.
n.d.   Dagomba Drum Histories. University Library, Legon, Ghana.

Tessman, G.
1913   *Die Pangwe.* Berlin.

Verger, B.
  1964   *Bahia and the West African Trade.* Ibadan.
  1968   *Flux et reflux de la traite des nègres entre le Golfe de Bénin et Bahia de Todos os Santos du XVIIe au XIXe siècle.* Paris.

Watt, I. P.
  1947   The Novel and Its Readers, 1719–1754. Fellowship dissertation, St. John's College, Cambridge.
  1957   *The Rise of the Novel: Studies in Defoe, Richardson and Fielding.* London.

Weber, M.
  1951   *The Religion of China.* Trans. H. Gerth and D. Martindale.
  [1916]   New York.

Wilks, I., et al.
  1986   *Chronicles from Gonja: A Tradition of West African Muslim Historiography.* Cambridge.

Yates, F. A.
  1966   *The Art of Memory.* London.

Index

abstraction, notion of, 5–6
abstract markers of time, 78
Abubakar, Mallam, 92
accountants, measurements by, 150–51
action, written versions as guides, 57–59, 60
Adams, Robert McCormick, 132
Africa: animals in myths, 77; cultural penetration of Europe, 153–54; daily well-being linked to religions, 102, 103; religious conversions, in oral beliefs, 122–23. *See also* West Africa
Āgamas: repetitive daily worship rites, 59–60; textual precepts and actual practices, 15–18
ahistorical analysis, 114
algebra, use of alphabetical symbols, 148
allegorical interpretations, of religious texts, 15–16, 60
alphabetical systems: and changes in systems of information, 9, 11–12, 128; Greece's contribution, 42; memorization of letters, 42; use of letters in abstract thought, 148
ancestors, in LoDagaa myth, 73, 103–4
ancestral figures found at archeological digs, interpretations of, 127
Ancient Art and Ritual (Harrison), 71
animals, in African myths, 77
anthropology, fieldwork and memory storage and retrieval, 141–42
Apocrypha, place in the Christian canon, 120
Arabic: knowledge of among slaves, 90–91; as written language for non-speakers, 4

archaeology, meanings of artifacts, 127
archives, in cultures with writing, 115
archi-writing, Derrida's model of speech and writing, 112
Art of Memory, The (Yates), 46
Asante people, Africa, stool histories, 19, 30–31
assonance, in Beowulf saga, 26
audiovisual communications, effect on the printed word, 155
Austen, Jane, 162
Australia, aborigines and Dreamtime, 77
authoritative versions, of oral ceremonial activities, 52, 55–56

back-to-the-Book movements, in Christianity and Islam, 15–16, 97, 104
Bacon, Francis, 114
Bagre myth, 103; narrative time and space, 71, 83; perceived standardized utterances and reality, 125–27; versions of and exactness of memory, 14, 36–40, 44, 45, 116–18; women's exclusion from stages of, 163
Bagre rituals, 49–51, 60; Black, 14, 37, 76; White, 37–40, 51, 71–78
Bahia, Brazil, slave revolts, 87–92, 94–95, 164–65
Baines, John, 12, 18–21
baptism, of slaves, 86–87
Barth, Fredrik, 10, 40, 54, 124
Bartlett, Frederic, 27, 35–36, 116, 117
beads, colored, as mnemonic aids, 32
Benedict, Ruth, 103
Beowulf saga, assonance in, 26

Bible, the: Jesus' words as precise or reconstructed, 43; preservation of written taboos found in Leviticus, 122; restriction of literacy to reading the text, 156, 160; Ten Commandments as religious canon, 119; use of Old Testament texts for modern day polygyny, 10; vagueness of time in Genesis, 77; view of Old Testament rituals as allegories, 60

birch-bark scrolls, Ojibway, 3

birth dates, importance in the concept of time, 79–80

Book, the: back-to-the-Book movements in Christianity and Islam, 15–16, 97, 104; Islam as a written creed, 100–101

book, the, as source of empowerment, 155–56

book burning, 157

bookkeeping, taught to women for practical reasons, 161

Book of Common Prayer, Anglican, 59

Boorstin, Daniel, 141

Bottéro, Jean, 147

boundaries, in oral and written religions, 101–2, 106, 121

bourgeoisie, petty, literacy among, 160

Bowra, C. M., 26–27

Bowser, Frederick, 87

Brahmanical tradition, 120

brain, the, influence of language on development, 133

Brazil. See Bahia, Brazil

Brennan, Teresa, 123

Bronze Age, property rights, 130

Buddhist diaspora, 153

bureaucracy, limitations in oral societies, 25

Cadres sociaux de la mémoire, Les, (Halbwachs), 117

calendar: in Central American graphic systems, 80; as measure of time, 65

calligraphy: in canonized texts, 120; eye and hand coordination, 136–37

Cambridge University, role in disputed Macedonian study, 158

canons: in oral cultures, 121–23; religious, source and transmission of written texts, 119–21; secular, role of the cultural elite, 121

Catholicism: baptism of slaves, 86–87; saints and cult movements, 102–3; and slaves' adherence to Islam, 91

censorship, in literate societies, 157–58

Chadwick, H. M., 70

characterization development, tightness or looseness in a narrative, 82

Childe, Gordon, 129

children: as audiences, 68–69; mimetic learning of languages, 28, 41

China: extension of ideology through script, 155–56; similarity of rites throughout, 41; women poets of the T'ang period, 161

chronicles, as early forms of history, 12, 19

Clanchy, M. T., 140

clans, migration accounts of space and time, 73, 81

classification systems, use by literate societies, 146

clay tablets, durability of, 145

clerks, as early specialists of the written word, 163

clocks, advent of and everyday consciousness of time, 66

Codere, Helen, 142

codes, legal, public display in the ancient world, 137

cognition, changes in, as an implication of literacy, 11–12

Cole, M., 28, 43, 154

collective memory, in oral cultures, 43–44

collegiality, through religious affiliations, 107

colonial period: manipulations of narratives to insure claims of rank and territory by conquered peoples, 75; spread of literacy, 134

commentaries, on canonized texts, 120

common lands, written laws and customary usage, 157

communications: audiovisual modes and the printed word, 155; control of, 1; intergenerational handing over of traditions, 13; in oral cultures, 27; relationship of iconography to other forms, 10–11; using written ritual texts, 48

communities, maroon, formed by runaway slaves in Brazil, 87, 168n3

contradiction, and logical relations, 142–43

convents, as sites for teaching young women, 160–61

conversion, religious: adherence to oral and religious creeds, 106–7; to African oral belief systems, 122–23

copying: constraints in rewriting canonical texts, 130; of texts as ancient reading and writing tools, 20; of texts for later use, 115–16
cosmology, in oral cultures, 71
crops: and sequential time, 72; yields as reason for nonreligious changes in oral cultures, 125–26
crossword puzzles, 147
cults, 93; rise and fall effect on oral religious canons, 121–22, 123; spread of in West Africa and Brazil, 102–3
culture(s): activities influenced by the written word, 18; differences and universal logic arguments, 5–6; *Geisteswissenschaft* views of, 22; influence of religions of conversion on nonliterate societies, 48–49; nonreligious adaptations in oral cultures, 124–25; power of literate societies over oral societies, 152–58; use of alphabetical systems, 9, 11–12, 128
cybernetics, use of term "writing" for programs, 115

Dakota Indians, Long Dog's Winter Count as form of time recording, 80
day, as a division of time, 79
de Castelnau, François, 96–97, 106
Declaration of the Rights of Man and of the Citizen, influence on slave revolts, 99–100
decontextualization of written languages, 6
deeds, land, as ownership documents in previously oral societies, 156–57
Defoe, Daniel, 64, 83
De la grammatologie (Derrida), 114–15
Derrida, Jacques, 2–3, 30, 109–18
determinacy, in technological changes, 135–36
Dewdney, Selwyn, 32–33
dialects: choice of one for written version of a language, 56; influence on oral nonreligious changes, 124; and national written languages, 21; proliferation in oral cultures, 42–43; and reproductions of myths, 40
dictionaries, as defining words, 144
discourse: in the dominant written language, 154; mystical and ordinary in LoDagaa funeral rites, 49–51; tables as analytic form, 146–47; uninterrupted monologues, 67–68
divination, interpretations of signs, 3

Domesday Book, effect on Norman law, 81
Douglass, Frederick, 154
dramatic performances, as uninterrupted narratives, 67
Dreamtime, in narratives of Australian Aborigines, 77
drum histories, of Dagomba, 19
drum recitals, of Japka narratives, 74
Durkheim, Émile, 24
dyslexia, cultural, and language of potential discourse, 154

East in the West, The (Goody), 1
Ebla, Syria, ancient archives of, 115–16, 145
education: European, early religious sites, 160–61; in oral cultures through verbal example, 24; role in information retrieval, 144–45
Egypt, early writing and chronological history, 18–21
Eisenstein, Elizabeth, 8, 22
Elias, Norbert, 123
Eliot, T. S., 8
elite, religious, role in preservation and transmission of canonical texts, 120–21
encyclopedias, as archives, 115
English language, use of Midlands dialect as written form, 56
epics: form of and oral narratives, 69–70; memory and recall in oral recitations, 13–15, 27; Yugoslav, 26, 70, 83
Essay Concerning Human Understanding, An (Locke), 64
Etienne, I., 93, 106
Euclidian geometry, 147–48
evangelization, as opposed to Catholic rituals, 60–61
Evensong, fixity of as written Anglican service, 38, 41
evidence, oral compared with written, 20

face-to-face oral transmissions, 142, 144. *See also* memory
farming systems, and religious rituals in precolonial Africa, 126
feminist movements, as literate attempts to empower the powerless, 162
Fiction and the Reading Public (Leavis), 8
Fielding, Henry, 66
field notes, and subsequent records in anthropological studies, 141–42
Filani, Mohammad-Abdullad, 96–97

Finnegan, Ruth, 22, 27, 70
firearms, protective written medicines against injury by, 92, 96
folktales: narrative structures of and audiences for, 68–69; recitational similarities, 41
forgetfulness, selective, possibilities of in oral cultures, 44
freedom, purchase of, by Bahian slaves, 89, 95, 170n17
French Revolution: influence on slave revolts, 99–100; influence on women authors, 162
Freud, Sigmund, 36
Freyre, Gilberto, 87, 90, 94
Fulani movement, ideological inspiration through fixed written texts, 104–5, 106
Fuller, C., 15–18, 59
funeral rites: Anglican services, 59; in China, 41; of the LoDagaa of northern Ghana, 49–51, 60

Gandah, Kum, 37, 73
Geisteswissenschaft, of a culture, 22
Gellner, Ernst, 3
gender, and canon, 129–30
genealogy, sequence of, 80–81
Genovese, E. D., 98–99
Giddens, Anthony, 123–24
Gilgamesh epic, 70
God(s)/god(s): concept of single deity and other supernatural agencies, 105–6; as failure in believers' daily lives, 102, 122; first man/men and knowledge received from deity/deities, 76–77; replacement of failed deities, 45; roles of lesser deities in oral religions, 102; speaking the words of, 35
Gonja kingdom, 81; narratives of Japka, Lord of the Towns, 74–76
grammar, in literate societies, 143–44
graphic communications: art as form of writing, 137; oral traditions and need for graphic representations, 25; relationship of iconography to other forms, 10–11; signs used to aid memories in oral cultures, 29; tables as analytic discourse, 146–47
Gray, Thomas, 110
Greece: alphabet attributed to, 139–40; attempts to forestall publication by Dr. Anastasia Karakasidou, 157–58; development of written history, 12
Greenway, J., 27

Haiti, slave uprisings, 89
Halbwachs, Maurice, 116, 117
Hammurabi, Code of, as public text, 137
hand and eye coordination, in writing, 136–37
handbook, ritual, as selective guide to action, 57–58, 60
Harrison, Jane, 71
Havelock, Eric, 138
health, African religions' link to, 102, 103
hierarchy: maintenance through knowledge of ancient texts, 20–21; of the written and the oral, 110–11
hieroglyphics, Lacan's comparison to coffee grounds, 113–14, 118
history: chronicles and genealogies, 12, 18–19; time's role in oral and written narratives, 80–83
Hocket, Charles, 132
hoe cultures, changes brought about by introducing the plow, 132–33
Homeric poems, 26, 34–35, 83
Hooke, S. H., 71
hour, as a division of time, 79

iconography, relationship to other forms of graphic communications, 10–11
icons, their perceived meanings, 127
illustration, as a means to describe action, 57
imitative faculty, attributed to men and apes, 29
India: as cultural power in East Asia, 152–53; early women writers, 129, 161; Tamil Nadu priests use of Kāmikōgama texts for Āgamas rituals, 16–17
Indic religions, sacred canons in, 120
informality, of ceremonies in oral rituals, 58–59
information retrieval: in alphabetical systems, 9, 128; of anthropological fieldwork, 141–42; education's role, 144–45; memory as storage center, 27–28, 29, 109, 144
ink, used in writing Qur'anic verses, drinking of for magico-religious purposes, 87, 93, 94, 96, 105
inscriptions: compared with temporary blackboard writings, 114; as public text, 137; in the structure of language, 112
intellect, changes through the manifold physical and material changes of writing, 133

Interface between the Written and the Oral, The (Goody), 109
intolerance, in literate religions, 106
intrasocietal dimension, of literacy in a society, 154
inventions, technological changes and sequential improvements, 135–36
Islam: concept of jinns as supernatural agencies, 105–6; influence on Brazilian slaves, 93–94, 96; influence on Mediterranean epics, 70; role in slave uprisings, 90–92, 97–98, 169n7; as a written creed, 100–101
Islamic literacy: knowledge of Arabic by African slaves, 90–91, 94; as restricted to religious texts, 4, 156, 160

Japka, Lord of the Towns, narrative versions in Gonja kingdom, 74–76
Jesus, words of as precise or reconstructed, 43
jinns, role in Islamic beliefs, 105–6
jokes, as uninterrupted monologues, 67
Jonathan Wild (Fielding), 66
Jousse, Marcel, 43

Kane, P. V., 17
Karakasidou, Anastasia, 157–58
Kellog, R., 44
Kent, R. K., 93, 169nn10, 11, 14
kinship: rights and land deeds in previously oral societies, 156–57; selection of in genealogical narratives, 80–81
knowledge: cumulative through written forms, 145–46; of God(s) received from first man/men, 76–77; hierarchy maintenance through access to ancient texts, 20–21; Islamic literacy among African slaves, 90–91, 94
Koster, Henry, 87
Kyeremateng, Alex, 56

Labov, William, 6
Lacan, J., 113–14, 118
land, written documents of ownership in previously oral societies, 156–57
language(s): as a codified method of manipulating an environment, 132; continuance of "dead" versions through written texts, 4, 20–21, 116; influence on human physiological makeup, 133; national written versions and regional dialects, 21, 56; proliferation of dialects in oral cultures, 42–43; silent thinking as linguistic activity, 149; as

supplanted by writing, 114–15; use of archaic forms in rituals, 74; use of Yoruba as lingua franca among Bahian slaves, 89, 94
Latin, as written language for non-speakers, 4
Leavis, Q. D., 8
lectures, as narratives, 67
legends, form of and oral narratives, 69
Lennox, Charlotte, 161
Lévi-Strauss, Claude, 5, 77, 123, 125, 142
Leviticus, preservation of written taboos, 122
Lévy-Bruhl, Lucien, 5, 142, 150
lexicons, as prerequisite of communications, 28
libraries, public, as sources of information for all, 159–60, 165
life cycles, in prophetic religions, 73
lineage rights, and land deeds in previously oral societies, 156–57
lists: ability to create through writing, 141, 146; as memory tests, 28
literacy: as historically limited to minority cultures, 133–34; intrasocietal dimensions within societies, 154; knowledge of Arabic among Bahian slaves, 90–92; modern universal approaches, 134; and power of the priesthood, 129; universal models sought by the underprivileged, 164; use of classical language texts among nonspeaking peoples, 4. *See also* Islamic literacy
literature: plays, 35, 48; poetry, 49, 161; as producing new writings, 128. *See also* novel, the
liturgical texts, written and oral versions, 15–18
Lloyd, Geoffrey, 147
location, narrative, of background in time and space, 82
Locke, John, 64
LoDagaa people (Ghana). *See* Bagre myth
logic(s): applied to cognitive activities of various cultures, 5–6, 81; and contradiction, 142–43; as reorganizing information, 147; of written cultures, 12
logocentrism, in Derrida's distinction between speech and writing, 110–11
logographs, learning process, 138–39
Lord, A. B., 13–15, 20, 26, 70
Luba people (Zaire), genealogies of founding ancestors, 31–32
Luria, Aleksandr, 6

Macedonia province, Greece, study of Slavic minorities, 157–58
magico-religious purposes: of books as viewed by the illiterate, 156; claimed protections against firearms, 92, 96; forms of writing, 87; ritual variations in neighboring precolonial African farming cultures, 125. *See also* ink
males, as historical guardians of religious canons, 129
Malinowski, Bronislaw, 75
malleability, and fixity of traditions, 9–25
manumission, effect on importing slaves, 87, 168n2
manuscript cultures, written texts and oral readings, 104–5
marriage rites, similarity of throughout China, 41
Martins, Francisco Gonçalves, 91–92
Master, life of the, annual cycles in prophetic religions, 73
material/immaterial dichotomy, in writing and speech, 137
mathematical tables: ability of nonreaders to learn, 148; as a technology of the intellect, 146–47
Mbudye historian rituals, and genealogies of Luba people's founding ancestors, 31–32
McKeon, Michael, 8
McLuhan, Marshall, 22
meaning, as seen by Derrida, 112–13
means-ends relationships: in ritual activities, 55; in technology, 136
memory: binary divisions in written and oral versions, 21–22; circular messages and final texts, 35–36, 117–18; role in epic oral recitations, 13–14; selective aspects of recall, 44, 116; standard list recollection tests, 28; as storage of information, 27–28, 29, 109, 144; use in rendering Āgamic texts, 16–17
mentalities, gap in, in Lévy-Bruhl's view, 149–50
Mesopotamia: development of written commercial records, 128, 138, 145; list-making activities, 146; memorization and writing exercises, 42
Mikra, as Jewish written law, 33
mimetic learning, of languages, 28, 41
mimetic representation, in funeral songs, 54–55
mind, human, interaction with the written word, 145–46
Mintz, Sidney, 9

Mishna, as Jewish oral law, 33, 34
mnemonic forms, of communications, 3, 29–30, 105, 113
Mohammad, as human agency for the Qur'an's sacred text, 120
monologues, and uninterrupted discourse, 67–68
monuments, as public displays of the written word, 19
moral junctions, generalizations of, 106–7
Mormon Bible, as text received through human agency, 120
mulatto slaves, viewed as adherents of Islamic beliefs, 98–99
Murasaki Shikibu, Lady, 161
mystical discourse, and everyday discourse in oral rites, 49
Mythologiques (Lévi-Strauss), 77
myths: form of and oral narratives, 69–70; as oral archives, 116–18; variations in, 10. *See also* Bagre myth

name(s), Christian, assigned to newly purchased slaves, 86–87
narrative: memory and recall in epic oral recitations, 14–15; tightness and looseness measures, 82–83; time in the written construction, 63–64; time's role in oral and written history, 80–83
Needham, Joseph, 140
New Guinea, variations in myth and ritual among adjacent societies, 10
newspaper narratives, time as part of the construction, 64
nonliterates, as oral communicators, 23
nonreligious changes, in oral cultures, 124–25
nonverbal acts, of ritual texts, 48, 57
novel, the: advent of printing and rise of the genre, 8; mental compositions compared with written versions, 48; particularization of time as background, 64; women as early readers and authors, 161–62

Ojibway people (Canada), use of mnemonic birch-bark scrolls, 32–33
Old Testament. *See* Bible, the
oral communications (orality): in societies with writing, 23–24, 100–101; systems of among men and animals, 132
oral cultures: effects of written land ownership documents, 156–57; variety of

in small geographic areas, 45; women's exclusion from many rituals, 162–63

oral recitations, disposability or malleability of earlier texts, 11, 25, 104–5

orthodoxy, rising from written versions of rites, 56, 59–60

Palmares, Brazil, as long-lasting runaway-slave community, 88

pantheons of deities, in West African religions, 103–4

Parkinson, J., 89–90

Parry, J., 20, 26, 43, 70

Parsons, Talcott, 25

perpetual services, as daily rituals not tied to specific occasions, 61–62

petitions, early written submissions in Egypt, 19–20

Philosophical and Political History of the Establishments and Commerce of the Europeans in the Two Indies (Raynal), 100

philosophy, Western: Derrida's deconstruction based on writing, 113–14; logocentric tradition in, 111; as skeptical of power distributions, 164

phonemes: comparison with graphic signs, 112; use in alphabets, 138

phonetic similarity, and substantive association, 114

Plato, 27, 111

plays: internalization of the written word, 48; need for memorization, 35

plot, tightness or looseness in a narrative, 82–83

plows, effects on hoe cultures, 132–33

poetry: use of rhyming schemes, 49; women poets in the T'ang period, 161

polygyny, use of Old Testament texts by Christian denominations, 10

power: literacy and the priesthood, 129; of literate societies over nonliterate cultures, 152–58

powerless, the, power gained through schooling and information sources, 158–65

precedents, in oral legal procedures, 25

precepts, sacred, and actual practices, 15–18

priesthood: intervention by and Protestant beliefs in direct communications, 60–61; power of through literacy, 129; role in preservation and transmission of canonical texts, 120–21, 128, 163

Primitive Song (Bowra), 26–27

Prince, H., 101

printing: advent of and subsequent importance, 3–4; effect on the rise of the novel, 8, 83–84; and spread of Protestantism, 61, 104, 160

proof, methods of, 147

Protestantism: and blacks in Brazil, 94; printing and availability of the written text, 61, 104, 160; rituals replaced by direct communication, 60–61

Psychopathology of Everyday Life, The (Freud), 36

quest, oral narratives as, 73, 76, 103

question and answer processes, in oral rituals, 52

Qur'an: Arabic as the written language, 4; memorization of texts in non-Arabic speaking countries, 34; Mohammad as human agency for the text, 120; restriction of literacy to reading the text, 156, 160; use of early premises in modern Islamic societies, 10

Rajasthani epic of Pabuji, 13–14

Rattray, R. S., 31

reading. *See* literacy

reading methods, effects on communications, 9

realism, and concept of time, 64

recall: in epic oral recitations, 14–15; as selective process, 116; verbatim, difficulty of, 42–43

recitation: disposability or malleability of earlier oral texts, 11, 25, 104–5; memory and recall in oral epics, 13–15, 27; of texts as ancient learning tool, 20; use of rhyme, 26–27, 41, 49, 53

recitativo, as form of oral ritual speaking, 53

references, to previous writing and current positions, 164

reflexivity, of written material and the writer, 148–49

rehearsal, ritual handbooks as orchestration of the written service, 60

Reisman, David, 27

religion(s): back-to-the-Book movements, 15–16, 97, 104; changes in beliefs in oral societies, 123–24; connections with literacy, 4; literacy restrictions, 156. *See also* Catholicism; Islam; Protestantism

Religion(s) of the Book: as dominant in sixteenth-century England, 134;

Religion(s) of the Book (*cont.*): and extension of colonial power, 155–56; Islam, 100–101; Torah, 119
Remembering (Bartlett), 27, 117
remembrance. *See* memory
reminiscences, as oral narratives, 67
repetition: of actions during written versions of ceremonies, 58–59; in oral performances of epics, 27; through recurring rites, 62
replication, role in the White Bague rituals, 72–73
retrieval, information. *See* information retrieval
review, as possible in the process of writing, 149–50
rhyme: as aid in similarities of song recitations, 41; recitativo form of oral ritual speaking, 53; use in oral performances of epics, 26–27; use in poetical schemes, 49
Rig Veda, 70, 127; mnemonic structure of, 26, 34, 43
Rise of the Novel, The (Watt), 8
rituals: consecutiveness of activities as aid to memory, 28; proper performance through written texts, 21; as uninterrupted narratives, 67; use of Kāmikōgama texts for Āgamas rituals, 16–17; variations in, 10; verbal and nonverbal acts of, 48. *See also* Bagre rituals
Rivers, W. H. R., 27, 110, 135
Robinson Crusoe (Defoe), 64–65, 68, 83–85
Rodrigues, Nina, 90–92, 96, 169n11
Rousseau, Jean-Jacques, 111, 161
runaway slaves, establishment of communities in Brazil, 87, 168n3
Rushdie, Salman, 157

Saint-Domingue, slave uprisings, 89
Sanskrit, as text language for rituals, 4, 16
Sappho, 129, 161
Saussure, Ferdinand, 111
Schipper, K., 58
Schmandt-Besserat, D., 128, 138
schools: in ancient Egypt, 20; in Europe, 160
schoolteachers, as early specialists of the written word, 163
science, changes in and dating of textbooks, 128
Science and Civilisation in China (Needham), 140

scribes: as early specialists of the written word, 163; role in transmitting traditions orally, 33–34
Scribner, S., 28, 34
script(s): cognitive operations compared with speech, 140–41; differences and technology levels, 145; extension of Chinese ideology through, 155–56; gradual development effect on malleability of traditions, 12; logographic forms of, 138–40; written, as a more formal version of oral proceedings, 53–54
scriptoria, as bastions for elitist cultures, 20–21
seasons, the, as sequential time, 72
seers, superhuman, in the Brahmanical tradition, 120
sequential activities: the seasons as in rituals, 72; in technological improvements, 135–36; as visible clues to ritual recollections, 28
sermons, as uninterrupted narratives, 67
Shakespearean canon, 121
shrines, religious, 102–4, 122
signification, as dependent on differences in communication, 112
signs: graphic, comparison with phonemes, 112; logograph meanings as same in different dialects or languages, 139; visual, interpretations of, 3
silent thinking, as linguistic activity, 149
singers, professional, of epic tales, 70
single-factor causation, as determining technological changes, 135–36
skepticism, writing as a continuing tradition, 164
slaves, New World/African affiliations and subsequent uprisings, 87–92, 94–95, 100, 164–65
Smith, Joseph, 120
Smith, R., 13–14
Smith, W. Robertson, 71
solitary activities, views of in oral cultures, 24
songs, funeral, topical matters incorporated into, 54
sonnets, mental compositions compared with written versions, 48
Soyinka, Wole, 153
Speaker, the, role in LoDagaa rites, 52–53, 126
speech: compared with cognitive operations in writing, 140–41; dependence

on verbal memory, 109; restrictions on meaning, 113

Spokesman, role in Asante stool history, 30–31

statement and repetition, in oral rituals, 52

Sterne, Laurence, 65–66

Stone, Lawrence, 80

stool histories, of Asante people, 19, 30–31

storage, information: anthropological fieldwork and later retrieval, 141–42; memory as source in oral cultures, 27–28, 29, 109, 144

storytelling, 66–67, 83

Street, Brian, 3, 4–5, 6, 7–8, 9–11

subgroups, in cultures with oral and written traditions, 23, 100–101

Sumerian, as written language in ancient Middle East, 116

sun, position of and time of day, 79

supernatural, the, as sources for written religious texts, 119–20

Sweetness and Power (Mintz), 9

syllogism, notion of, as dependent on introduction of writing, 6

symbolic logic, use of alphabetical symbols, 148

syncretism, of slaves' beliefs in Brazil, 93, 101

tables, as analytic discourse in written forms, 146–47

taboos, transitory nature in oral cultures, 122

Tale of Genji, The (Murasaki), 161

Taoist ceremonies, 58

tape recorders, 53; comparison of oral texts over time and place, 126; subsequent transcriptions, 47, 142

technology, use of the term, 132–33, 135

temples, as centers of written knowledge, 21

Ten Commandments, as religious canon, 119

tests, functions of the questions and questionnaires, 6

text(s): ancient Egyptian law documents, 19; arguments on immutability of, 9–10; conservative function of sacred writings, 15–16; contrast between religious texts and utterances, 127–28; creation by utterance and fixation through writing, 104–5; liturgical versions in written and oral renditions,

15–18; use of classical languages, 4, 116; written religions' relationships defined by, 101

then and now, merging of in LoDagaa narratives, 77

thinking, when writing and speaking, 149

Thomas Aquinas, 144

time: as conceived in spoken narrations, 66–78; concept in the written form, 63–66; importance in *Robinson Crusoe,* 64–65; and narrative in oral and written history, 80–83; sequential time in the White Bagre, 72; telling of in oral and written narratives, 78–80

Tiv genealogies, West Africa, 81

tokens, commercial, and development of writing, 138

Tom Jones (Fielding), 66

topical matters, in funeral songs, 54–55

Torah, the, as religious canon, 119

Toronto School, studies on writing's influence on human life, 111

Toussaint-Louverture, 89, 99, 100, 164

trace, memory: in oral transmissions, 116, 144; writing as seen connected to, 115

traditions, fixity of and malleability, 9–25

tribal affiliations, and slave disunity, 107

Tristram Shandy (Sterne), 65–66, 68

underprivileged, the, as ruled by the literate, 163–65

unity, and oral composition, 13

universalism, in literate religions, 106

universe, views of the, binary divisions in folk and scholarly versions, 22

uprisings, slave, 87–92, 94–95, 100, 164–65

variations: in the Bagre myth, 14, 36–40, 44, 45, 116–18; in circular message text tests, 35–36, 117–18; curtailment of in written ritual versions, 54

Vedas: Rig Veda, 26, 34, 43, 70, 127; source of in the Brahmanical tradition, 120

verbal acts, of ritual texts, 48

verbatim memory, in ceremonial activities, 55

verbatim repetition, in epic oral recitations, 13–14

Vindication of the Rights of Women, A (Wollstonecraft), 162

Vygotsky, L. S., 6

Watt, Ian, 3–5, 8–9, 15, 22, 64
Weber, Max, 25, 123
well-being, daily, African oral religions link to, 103
West Africa: contact with by Bahian slaves, 91, 169n8; Guinea coast as source for Spain's New World slaves, 86; percentage of slaves in countries of, 107; Yoruba people as slaves, 89, 91–93, 97
wills, texts in ancient Egypt, 20
wives, education of merchant and tradesmen classes, 161
Wollstonecraft, Mary, 162
women: contributions as writers, 2, 161–62; limited roles as historical guardians of religious canons, 129–30; literacy among, 160–63
worship, daily, as repetitive ceremonies, 59–60
writing: and anticanonization, 130; as Crusoe's means to conquer time, 82–83; early forms restricted by religious considerations, 11–12; interaction with the human mind, 145–46; as magico-religious exercise, 87; monopolization by early priesthoods, 128; and orthodoxy of a written version, 56; reflexivity of material and the writer, 148–49; as substitute for descriptive language, 114–15. *See also* literacy; text(s)
Writing and Difference (Derrida), 113
written compositions, and notion of unity, 13
written word, the: arguments on immutability of texts, 9–10; compared with oral compositions, 48–49; Derrida on the oral and, 109–18

Yates, Frances, 46
Yoruba people, Africa: as Bahian slaves and as returnees, 89, 97; as principal participants in Bahian slave revolts, 91–93
Yugoslav epics, 26, 70, 83